3rd Grade FAST Test Prep Florida 2024-2025 Reading

- 📖 **Mastering Your Study Plan**: Learn how to create a personalized study strategy that suits your unique needs, maximizing efficiency and reducing wasted time.
- 🧠 **Enhancing Cognitive Performance**: Explore effective techniques to improve memory, deepen understanding, and solidify knowledge for long-term retention.
- ⏰ **Achieving Balance**: Apply smart time management methods to maintain a balance between study, work, and personal life, fostering a sustainable and healthy routine.
- 🏆 **Managing Stress Effectively**: Overcome exam anxiety with mindfulness, relaxation techniques, and resilience-building exercises to stay calm and focused when it matters most.
- 📘 **Practicing for Success**: Understand the value of practice exams, sample questions, and mock tests, and learn how to analyze your performance to identify areas for growth.

Disclaimer of Liability:

This book is intended to provide readers with general information on various topics discussed within its content. It is sold with the understanding that neither the author nor the publisher is offering professional advice, including but not limited to legal, medical, or other specialized fields. Readers should seek the services of qualified professionals when professional assistance is needed.

Despite diligent efforts to ensure accuracy, errors or inaccuracies may be present. The author and publisher disclaim any liability for any loss or damage, whether direct or indirect, that may result from the use or reliance on the information in this book. This includes any potential loss or harm arising from the content provided.

The information in this book is provided "as is," without any warranties regarding its completeness, accuracy, usefulness, or timeliness. Readers are encouraged to consult certified experts or professionals for the most current and reliable information.

The viewpoints expressed in this book do not represent those of any specific organization or professional entity. Any perceived offenses towards individuals or groups are entirely unintentional.

TABLE OF CONTENT

STUDY GUIDE	4
Chapter 1: Overview of the FAST Reading Test in Florida	7
Chapter 2: Word Recognition and Phonics	12
Chapter 3: Development of Vocabulary	17
Chapter 4: Determining the Key Concept and Specifics	22
Chapter 5: Inference and Conclusion-Making	28
Chapter 6: Comprehending Story Structure	34
Chapter 7: Recognizing Textual Elements	40
Chapter 8: Information Comparison and Contrast	45
Understanding Cause and Effect in Chapter 9	50
Chapter 10: Text Summarization	55
Chapter 11: Examining Personas and Their Qualities	61
Chapter 12: Figurative Language Interpretation	66
Chapter 13: Examining Texts with Information	72
How to Respond to Multiple-Choice Questions in Chapter 14	78
Chapter 15: Concluding Recap and Exam-Taking Advice	83
Practice Questions and Answers Explanations Latest Edition	89

STUDY GUIDE

Chapter 1: Introduction to the Florida FAST Reading Assessment

- Overview of the test format and expectations.
- Key skills required for success in 3rd-grade reading.
- How to approach the test and manage time effectively.

Chapter 2: Phonics and Word Recognition

- Understanding the importance of phonics in reading.
- Common phonetic patterns and how to recognize them.
- Practice with decoding and blending sounds in words.

Chapter 3: Vocabulary Development

- Importance of vocabulary in reading comprehension.
- Strategies for learning new words (context clues, root words, affixes).
- Activities to build and reinforce vocabulary knowledge.

Chapter 4: Identifying Main Idea and Details

- What is the main idea of a passage?
- How to identify supporting details.
- Practice with reading short passages and finding the main idea and key details.

Chapter 5: Making Inferences and Drawing Conclusions

- Understanding what an inference is.
- How to use clues from the text to make inferences.
- Practice exercises on making inferences based on short reading passages.

Chapter 6: Understanding Story Structure

- Elements of a story (beginning, middle, end).
- Identifying characters, setting, problem, and solution.
- Analyzing the plot of a story through practice exercises.

Chapter 7: Understanding Text Features

- Overview of text features (headings, captions, illustrations, etc.).
- How text features support comprehension.
- Practice identifying and using text features to understand the text better.

Chapter 8: Comparing and Contrasting Information

- Understanding comparison and contrast.
- How to find similarities and differences in texts.
- Practice exercises comparing characters, events, or ideas in a text.

Chapter 9: Understanding Cause and Effect

- Explanation of cause and effect relationships.
- Identifying causes and effects in reading passages.
- Practice with cause-and-effect scenarios.

Chapter 10: Summarizing Texts

- How to summarize a story or informational text.
- Key points to include in a summary (main idea, important details).
- Practice summarizing short stories and passages.

Chapter 11: Analyzing Characters and Their Traits

- Understanding character traits (how characters feel, think, and act).
- How to describe characters based on their actions and words.
- Practice analyzing characters in various reading passages.

Chapter 12: Understanding Figurative Language

- Introduction to figurative language (similes, metaphors, idioms).
- Recognizing figurative language in texts.
- Exercises identifying figurative language in sentences.

Chapter 13: Reading Informational Texts

- Characteristics of informational texts (articles, expository writing, etc.).
- How to identify key ideas and details in informational texts.
- Practice with reading and answering questions about informational passages.

Chapter 14: Answering Multiple-Choice Questions

- How to approach multiple-choice questions in the test.
- Strategies for eliminating incorrect answers and choosing the best one.
- Practice with sample multiple-choice reading questions.

Chapter 15: Final Review and Test-Taking Tips

- Review of key reading strategies and skills.
- Tips for staying calm and focused during the test.
- Practice tests and exercises to prepare for the final assessment.

Chapter 1: Overview of the FAST Reading Test in Florida

A vital component of Florida's educational system, the Florida FAST Reading Assessment was created to assess and encourage children' reading development. It tests critical reading abilities and makes sure that kids are on track to meet state literacy standards, making it a significant turning point in the educational path for third graders. Students, parents, and teachers can successfully manage the test's hurdles if they have a clear understanding of the assessment's goal and how to prepare for it.

1.1 The Florida FAST Reading Assessment Overview

The Florida Standards Assessments (FSA), which include the Florida Assessment of Student Thinking (FAST), are intended to assess students' knowledge and abilities in accordance with the Florida State Standards. The FAST Reading Assessment is designed to gauge third-grade children' reading performance and is in line with Florida's demanding academic standards. "Reading proficiency" in this sense refers to the capacity to comprehend, evaluate, and interpret a variety of writings, including both fiction and educational books.

The FAST Reading Assessment measures third-grade students' reading comprehension abilities, their capacity to comprehend important concepts and details, their ability to draw conclusions, and their ability to evaluate textual organization. This evaluation aids in determining if kids are on course for academic achievement, especially in terms of becoming ready for the more complex reading skills needed in later grades.

1.2 The FAST Assessment's Objective
The following goals guided the creation of the FAST Reading Assessment:

Assessing Reading Proficiency: The FAST Reading Assessment's main goal is to gauge a third-grader's reading ability, specifically in terms of comprehension and text analysis. Being proficient in reading is essential for success in all courses, not just language arts, as it is a fundamental talent.

The FAST test assists parents and teachers in determining if students possess the abilities necessary for academic success.

Finding Improvement Needs: The evaluation offers insightful data regarding particular areas where students could require more assistance. The findings of the FAST exam can help teachers design focused interventions to meet the needs of students who are having trouble with certain reading abilities, such as drawing conclusions, comprehending the main idea, or recognizing cause and effect.

Ensuring Reading Readiness: In order to advance to the fourth grade in Florida, third graders must pass the reading section of the FAST exam. This guarantees that pupils have the abilities needed to complete the increasingly difficult reading tasks they will face in the later grades. Thus, the FAST Reading Assessment serves as a crucial benchmark for assessing a student's readiness to advance in their academic career.

Encouraging State Accountability: The state uses the FAST Reading Assessment results to hold schools responsible for the kind of instruction they deliver. Schools with high reading scores are commended for their achievements, while those with poor scores can get more funding or direction to help students achieve better results.

Monitoring Student Development Over Time: The FAST test is a component of a system intended to monitor students' academic development over time. Teachers can track progress, spot patterns, and modify their lessons to better suit the requirements of their pupils by evaluating reading proficiency at various points in a child's schooling.

1.3 The FAST Reading Assessment's Structure

Comprising numerous components, the FAST Reading Assessment is intended to assess a range of skills that pupils must acquire. To help pupils face the test with confidence, it is crucial to acquaint them with its structure and expectations. An outline of the main elements of the FAST Reading Assessment may be found below.

Reading Comprehension Reading comprehension is one of the main components of the test. Students will read brief excerpts from both factual and imaginative books and respond to questions about the material. Students may be asked to identify the passage's core idea, supporting information, plot points, character traits, and other important ideas in these questions. The purpose of reading comprehension questions is to evaluate a student's ability to comprehend and evaluate the material in its entirety as well as their capacity to draw conclusions from what they have read.

Contextual Vocabulary: The purpose of the vocabulary questions is to gauge how effectively students comprehend the meaning of terms within a paragraph. Students may come across vocabulary that they may not be familiar with, and they will have to use the passage's context to determine what these words imply. Vocabulary questions assess students' knowledge of word structures, prefixes, and suffixes as well as their capacity to infer meaning from the surrounding text.

Literary Analysis: Students are expected to examine the plot, characters, setting, conflict, and resolution of fiction books. Students are frequently asked to draw conclusions about the intentions and deeds of characters as well as pinpoint significant passages in the narrative that add to the overall meaning of the work in order to complete literary analysis questions. Additionally, students might be requested to contrast and compare certain characters or plot points in the narrative.

Informational Text Analysis: Students are supposed to examine the organization of non-fiction texts and pinpoint important elements. These texts could be articles that provide information, directions, or explanations. Students must be able to recognize the key ideas and illustrative elements as well as comprehend how the author arranges the material. Additionally, they will be asked to identify the text's goal and the target audience.

1.4 Time and Format of the Test

A multiple-choice section and a text-based response section are the two main components of the third-grade FAST Reading Assessment. The purpose of each segment is to evaluate various facets of reading comprehension.

Multiple-choice questions assess students' comprehension of the text and their capacity to identify the right response from a list of options. The core idea, vocabulary, inferences, and understanding of particular details may all be the subject of multiple-choice questions. From the available alternatives, students will select the best response.

Text-Based Response: Students must write a response in this section of the test based on a brief paragraph they have read. Students are usually asked to summarize the reading, draw conclusions, or explain their rationale in these responses. Students' ability to articulate their views clearly and substantiate them with textual evidence is evaluated in the text-based answer part.

Students should anticipate spending between 60 to 90 minutes finishing the complete test, while the precise amount of questions and the time allotted for it may change from year to year. Although the test is significant, pupils are not expected to complete it quickly. Students are expected to accurately and thoughtfully display their reading abilities.

1.5 Getting Ready for the FAST Reading Exam

Long before the actual test, students start preparing for the FAST Reading Assessment. Instead than trying to prepare for the test at the last minute, it is crucial that students continuously practice and improve their reading abilities throughout the year. The following are some methods that can assist students in efficiently getting ready for the test:

Read Frequently: Reading frequently is the best strategy to get ready for the FAST Reading Assessment. Students should be encouraged to read a range of literature, including poetry, non-fiction, fiction, and educational materials. Reading extensively will improve their vocabulary and comprehension abilities while also acquainting them with various text genres and structures.

Practice Reading Comprehension: To assist pupils in improving their reading comprehension abilities, assign them practice passages. Ask students to respond to questions that assess their comprehension of the passage's core idea, conclusions, and important details. As they read, encourage them to underline or highlight significant passages.

Develop Vocabulary: Encourage kids to acquire new words and practice identifying unfamiliar phrases by using context clues. This will help them increase their vocabulary. Make vocabulary and definition flashcards or assign kids to keep a vocabulary notebook to record new words they come across while reading.

Talk about Books: Have frequent conversations with kids regarding the books and texts they are reading. Pose queries that encourage them to consider themes, setting, characters, and plot. Students should be encouraged to discuss their thoughts and opinions as well as draw connections between various books.

Take Practice Exams: To help students feel less anxious and more confident, it is crucial to acquaint them with the format of the test. To assist students get comfortable answering multiple-choice questions and composing text-based responses, use practice exams to mimic the test-taking process.

Chapter 2: Word Recognition and Phonics

Particularly for third-grade students getting ready for the Florida FAST Reading Assessment, phonics and word recognition are fundamental abilities for reading growth. Stronger understanding and fluency are facilitated by knowing how to decode words and identify recognizable linguistic patterns. The significance of phonics in reading, the ways in which phonics aids in word recognition, and useful techniques for improving these abilities are the main topics of this chapter.

2.1 Phonics' Significance in Reading

The link between letters and sounds, which serves as the foundation for word decoding, is known as phonics. For third-graders to read fluently and comprehend the texts they come across in class and on tests like the FAST Reading Assessment, they must become proficient in phonics. In order for kids to read accurately and efficiently, phonics helps them break down difficult words into smaller, more accessible parts.

One of the first steps to becoming a proficient reader is learning phonics. Students come across increasingly difficult literature as they move through the early stages. Students must be able to identify letter patterns, comprehend how those patterns sound, and use that understanding to interpret unknown words in order to decode these texts. This process is made possible by phonics education, which is particularly important in grades K–3, as students go from learning to read to reading to learn.

Writing and spelling are also impacted by phonics. Students can enhance their spelling abilities by comprehending the relationships between sounds and symbols, which in turn promotes writing clarity and fluency. This ability influences how students interact with written content and effectively communicate their ideas, making it a crucial part of literacy development.

2.2 How Word Recognition Is Assisted by Phonics

The capacity to rapidly and precisely identify words is known as word recognition. Students who are proficient in phonics are able to detect words more quickly because they have a mental bank of known letter patterns and sounds. The two main elements of word recognition are sight words and decoding.

Decoding: Decoding is the process of sounding out a word using phonics knowledge. When a learner comes across the word "cat," for instance, they can decode it using their understanding of the distinct sounds of "c," "a," and "t." Phonics training, which teaches pupils to break words down into syllables and separate sounds, is crucial to decoding.

Words that pupils instantly recognize without needing to hear them out are known as sight words. These words are challenging to interpret because they frequently exhibit irregularities or deviate from standard phonetic patterns. Students must commit sight words to memory, such as "the," "said," "where," and "could." Although phonics training aids in pupils' awareness of frequent patterns, sight word memorization is equally essential for effective reading. Students can concentrate on understanding because they will need to use less cognitive energy when reading if they can recognize more sight words quickly.

The cornerstone of word recognition, which helps pupils read smoothly and comprehend what they read, is made up of sight word recognition and decoding. By giving kids the means to deconstruct words and understand their context, phonics aids in the development of these abilities.

2.3 Essential Phonics Competencies for Third Graders

It is expected of third-graders to have a firm knowledge of phonics. In order to read more difficult texts, they need be able to employ phonics techniques, identify a broad range of word patterns, and decode both regular and irregular words. For third graders, the following crucial phonics abilities are necessary:

Combining distinct sounds to create words is known as "blending sounds." Students should be able to mix the letters "s," "t," "r," "a," and "i," for instance, to form the word "straw." This ability is essential for fluency because it enables pupils to read words naturally and fluidly. By the third grade, pupils ought to be able to combine sounds to form increasingly difficult words, like "consonant blends" (e.g., "pl," "str," and "cr").

Sound Segmentation: The opposite of blending is sound segmentation. It entails dissecting a word into its constituent sounds. The word "dog" can be broken down into /d/, /o/, and /g/, for example. Students in the third grade should be able to segment and mix sounds in a variety of word kinds. Spelling and reading comprehension both benefit from this ability.

Identifying R-controlled Vowels: When a vowel is followed by the letter "r," it changes its sound composition. Common r-controlled vowel patterns include "ar," "or," "ir," "er," and "ur" (e.g., "car," "fork," "bird," "her," and "burn"). Students in the third grade should be able to recognize and accurately read words with r-controlled vowels.

Recognizing Diphthongs and Vowel Digraphs: A digraph is a pair of vowels that combine to form a single sound, like "ai" in "rain" or "ea" in "seat." Similar in sound, diphthongs combine two vowel sounds, such as "oy" in "boy" or "ou" in "cloud." Reading both known and unknown words requires an understanding of these patterns.

The third grade is a good time for kids to learn about common prefixes and suffixes, which are words that are added to root words to alter their meaning. The prefix "un-" turns "happy" into "unhappy," for instance, whereas the suffix "-ness" turns "kind" into "kindness." Understanding these typical affixes aids pupils in identifying and decoding increasingly difficult words.

Silent Letters: Students also need to be familiar with silent letters. In words like "write," "knife," or "doubt," some letters are not uttered. Students in the third grade should work on reading and identifying words that contain silent letters.

2.4 Methods for Teaching Word Recognition and Phonics

Teaching phonics well is essential to assisting pupils in becoming proficient readers. To encourage the development of phonics and word recognition, teachers can employ a range of tactics. Here are a few methods for developing these abilities:

clear Phonics Instruction: A methodical, clear approach to teaching phonics is recommended. Letter-sound correlations should be taught to students, beginning with the most basic patterns and working their way up to more intricate ones. These correlations can be taught by teachers using phonics worksheets, charts, and flashcards.

Interactive Reading Activities: Students can engage in hands-on phonics practice with interactive reading activities like "word sorts" and "sound hunts." For instance, teachers can assign students a list of words and ask them to arrange them according to common phonetic characteristics (e.g., "long a" sounds like "cake," "name," and "game"). Students learn to identify patterns and hone their word recognition abilities with these exercises.

Reading Aloud and Shared Reading: By reading aloud to their pupils, teachers can set an example of fluent reading while highlighting phonics rules and word patterns. Students can practice phonics skills together through shared reading exercises, in which they read aloud with the teacher.

Phonics Games: Playing phonics games is an enjoyable method to practice phonics abilities. In a game-like environment, games such as "phoneme pop," "word building," and "phonics bingo" help students use their phonics skills and recognize word patterns. These enjoyable exercises inspire students to consider words critically.

Contextual Learning: Students can better apply what they have learned to real-world reading scenarios when phonics is taught in a story, song, or poem. By relating phonics knowledge to authentic reading situations, contextual learning improves word recognition and comprehension.

Word Walls: A word wall is a grouping of often encountered high-frequency words or phonetic patterns. In order to encourage students to use word walls when reading and writing, teachers might put them up in the classroom. Throughout the academic year, this tool aids in the reinforcement of phonics and word recognition abilities.

Repeated Practice: The secret to improving fluency is consistent, spaced repetition. Students improve their ability to recognize words and use their decoding techniques by regularly practicing phonics abilities through a variety of exercises.

2.5 Evaluating Word Recognition and Phonics

Frequent assessments are necessary to make sure that pupils are acquiring good phonics and word recognition abilities. All of these evaluations, whether formal or informal, offer insightful commentary on a student's development. Typical evaluation instruments include the following:

Phonics Screeners: These tests concentrate on a student's capacity to recognize sounds and decode words. Usually including reading lists of words or phrases that contain specific phonetic patterns, phonics screeners can be given one-on-one.

During a reading session, a running record is a tool used to evaluate a student's word recognition and fluency. It gives teachers information about a pupil's phonics and word recognition skills by assisting them in identifying which words the student can recognize right away and which ones they find difficult.

Spelling Tests: Given the tight relationship between spelling and phonics, spelling tests can be a useful tool for evaluating a student's comprehension of phonetic patterns. Students may be asked to spell words that have particular phonetic components, such as r-controlled vowels or vowel digraphs.

Word Recognition Fluency: Tests of fluency evaluate how rapidly and precisely pupils can identify words. Students may be required to read word lists or brief texts as part of timed exercises. Determining how automatic and effortless word recognition has become is the aim.

Chapter 3: Development of Vocabulary

Building one's vocabulary is essential to literacy and a major indicator of academic achievement. A broad and varied vocabulary is essential for third graders getting ready for the Florida FAST Reading Assessment, both for reading comprehension and for general learning in all subject areas. This chapter examines the value of vocabulary, its effects on reading comprehension, and practical methods for fostering vocabulary growth in early students.

3.1 The Value of Developing Vocabulary

The collection of words that kids can comprehend and utilize in speaking, reading, and writing is referred to as their vocabulary. The acquisition of vocabulary is particularly important for third-grade kids as they move from "learning to read" to "reading to learn." Students' understanding and academic achievement are significantly impacted by their capacity to comprehend and employ a broad variety of words as they come across increasingly complicated texts in the third grade.

Reading comprehension and vocabulary knowledge are strongly correlated, according to research. Students are more likely to comprehend the material they are reading when they are aware of the definitions of the terms they are using. Students may find it difficult to comprehend a text's primary concepts, themes, or specifics if they lack a strong vocabulary basis. Therefore, expanding one's vocabulary is essential for writing and critical thinking in addition to improving reading comprehension.

Students are supposed to have a strong vocabulary base by the third grade. This makes it possible for kids to interact with more complex subject matter, comprehend age-appropriate materials, and articulate their thoughts more clearly. Apart from decoding words and identifying word patterns, a robust vocabulary facilitates fluent reading by enabling pupils to focus more on understanding the meaning of a text and less on word decoding.

3.2 The Relationship Between Reading Comprehension and Vocabulary
The ability to comprehend, interpret, and evaluate literature is known as reading comprehension. Developing one's vocabulary is essential to this process. Students must have skills for comprehending and retaining new

terms when they come across them. Students may find it difficult to make connections between concepts and deduce meaning from the text if they lack a strong vocabulary.

When a third-grader encounters a word like "turbulent," for example, they might not understand what it means. They can, however, infer its meaning by employing techniques like word parts (prefixes, suffixes, or root words) and by comprehending the context in which it appears. Students that have a large vocabulary are better able to deduce meaning from context, which enhances comprehension.

Receptive and expressive vocabulary are the two essential categories of vocabulary.

The words that pupils comprehend when they hear or read them are referred to as receptive vocabulary. The main ways that this kind of vocabulary is developed are through reading and speaking.

The terms that kids can employ in both writing and speaking are referred to as expressive vocabulary. For clear communication, expressive vocabulary is just as necessary as receptive vocabulary, which usually grows more quickly.

The development of both expressive and receptive vocabularies is necessary to improve reading comprehension. While expressive vocabulary enables pupils to successfully communicate their thoughts, receptive vocabulary aids in word decoding and context understanding.

3.3 Types of Vocabulary When it comes to vocabulary development, it's critical to differentiate between the many word types that pupils will come across and must comprehend. These consist of:

Tier 1 Words: From a young age, children are exposed to these simple, commonplace words. They don't need much teaching and are widely used in spoken language. One can think of words like "dog," "happy," "eat," or "run." Even though they serve as the cornerstone of a child's vocabulary, these words are insufficient for third-grade academic performance.

Tier 2 Words: These are less common in casual speech and are more scholarly in nature. They are crucial for reading comprehension, though, because they can be found in a variety of literature. Tier 2 terms are frequently used in a variety of contexts and have multiple meanings. Among them are "analyze," "determine," "adapt," and "contrast." Since they will come across these words in reading texts from a variety of topic areas, third graders should be introduced to them.

Tier 3 Words: These words are rarely used outside of specialized settings and are subject-specific. Tier 3 words include, for instance, "photosynthesis" in science, "germinate" in biology, and "democracy" in social studies. While less crucial for general reading comprehension, some words are crucial for subject-area learning.

Students should concentrate on increasing their Tier 2 vocabulary in the third grade since it will help them understand texts from a variety of subject areas. Giving pupils several exposures and usage chances is essential while teaching Tier 2 vocabulary.

3.4 Vocabulary Teaching Techniques Good vocabulary training aids students in remembering and using words in many settings in addition to helping them comprehend them. The following are research-backed vocabulary-building techniques:

Explicit Vocabulary training: Students can methodically increase their comprehension of new words through direct vocabulary training. This includes:

Word Lists: At the start of each week or subject, teachers might introduce students to particular vocabulary words. To assist pupils grasp the meaning and context of words, they can be explained, discussed, and utilized in sentences.
Word maps are a visual aid that students can use to investigate a word's definition, synonyms, antonyms, and related terms. This method fosters word connections and helps pupils grasp terminology more deeply.
Contextual Learning: Students learn how words work in sentences when they are taught vocabulary in context. Students learn words by seeing them used in context, not by memorizing separate definitions. When reading a story, for instance, teachers can point out vocabulary that students may not be familiar with, define them, and talk about how the words add to the story's meaning.

Thematic Vocabulary Instruction: Students learn how words connect to one another when vocabulary words are grouped thematically, by theme or subject. For example, during an animal lesson, students may be exposed to terms like "habitat," "predator," "ecosystem," and "migration." By relating new words to existing information, this method aids pupils in developing a more comprehensive conceptual grasp.

Word Walls: Usually concentrating on high-frequency or thematic vocabulary, a word wall is a group of words that are hung on classroom walls. Word walls serve as a reference tool for reading and writing assignments and provide pupils with a visual reminder of the terms they are learning. It is possible to encourage students to use these words in their writing and speech.

Using Multiple Exposures: In order for students to really understand a word, they must come across it several times in various settings. Writing, activities, conversations, and reading can all help achieve this. Students are more likely to remember and use terms when they are used in speaking and writing exercises.

Morphological Awareness: Students can learn the meaning of new words by being taught about word origins, prefixes, and suffixes. For instance, knowing that the prefix "un-" denotes "not" can aid pupils in comprehending terms like "unhappy" and "unfair." Even if students have never heard of a word before, morphological education aids in their decoding.

Games and Interactive Activities: Making learning enjoyable and memorable for pupils is achieved by involving them in vocabulary games or activities. Games such as "Jeopardy," "Vocabulary Bingo," and "Word of the Day" offer chances for active participation and repetition. Students can use new vocabulary to construct phrases, match words with definitions, or guess meanings in groups.

Reading Aloud: Students are exposed to a diverse vocabulary when they are read aloud to. Teachers might pause while reading to help pupils understand the meanings of challenging words and phrases. Additionally, reading aloud demonstrates pronunciation and fluency, both of which are critical for word recognition.

3.5 Evaluation of Vocabulary Growth
There are several ways to evaluate vocabulary:

Chapter 4: Determining the Key Concept and Specifics

The capacity to recognize a text's core concept and supporting information is one of the most important reading comprehension skills. This ability is crucial for success on the Florida FAST Reading Assessment since it enables students to comprehend a text's main idea and the evidence that supports it. This chapter examines the significance of recognizing the primary concept and supporting facts in a passage, their interrelationships, and techniques that can help third-grade students become proficient in this area.

4.1 Comprehending the Primary Concept

A text's core idea is the primary point or most significant message that the writer is attempting to get across. It serves as the text's main topic and usually provides an answer to the query, "What is this passage about?" For third-graders to comprehend what they are reading, they must be able to identify the primary theme. Students may find it difficult to understand the text if they don't understand the main idea since they won't understand what the author is attempting to say.

The opening sentence of a paragraph, the last sentence, or even the passage's title contain the major concept. The fundamental idea of longer works is frequently stated clearly in the opening and conclusion and backed up by specifics in the body of the work. The fundamental notion, however, may occasionally be implied—that is, not explicitly stated—but rather deduced from the information presented.

Gaining a thorough grasp of the core idea is essential for third-grade students getting ready for the Florida FAST Reading Assessment because it makes the material easier to arrange and comprehend. When responding to comprehension questions, students can concentrate on the most crucial elements by being able to discern the core concept from supporting details.

4.2 How Details Help to Support the Main Idea

Supporting details are the facts, illustrations, or descriptions that aid in elaborating, describing, or reaffirming the major idea, which is the primary topic or message. These specifics offer a greater comprehension of the core idea by supporting the author's major claim with facts.

For instance, the primary point in a chapter discussing the advantages of exercise would be, "Exercise is important for staying healthy." Examples of supporting details could be "It helps improve heart health," "It boosts mood and energy levels," or "Exercise strengthens muscles." The primary notion would be ambiguous or unsupported in the absence of these illustrative elements.

Since supporting elements give readers the background and elaboration they need to properly understand a paragraph, identifying and comprehending them is just as crucial as identifying the main concept. Students must be able to identify the main idea and the specific elements that support it in order to pass the Florida FAST Reading Assessment.

4.3 The Connection Between the Details and the Main Idea

Together, the primary idea and illustrative details form a logical and intelligible passage. The details add depth and clarity to the writing by building upon the main idea, which forms its foundation. This relationship can be viewed as a structure, with the supporting elements serving as the walls and roof and the primary idea as the framework.

Students must actively seek out details that support the primary theme while they read. They must also be able to distinguish between non-essential details—which offer supplementary information without immediately bolstering the core argument—and crucial details, which directly support the main idea.

In certain texts, particularly those that are more complicated, the reader may need to draw conclusions from the text's hints in order to determine the core theme and supporting facts. For instance, in a chapter that describes a beach trip, the primary concept would be about how much fun and relaxation the trip would be, with supporting details like descriptions of having a picnic, swimming in the water, or playing in the sand.

4.4 Methods for Determining the Primary Concept

Students in the third grade can utilize a variety of techniques to help them determine a text's core concept. Here are some useful strategies teachers might employ to help pupils navigate this process.

Search for the Topic Sentence: Usually found at the front of a paragraph, the topic sentence will explicitly explain the key concept. For longer sections, the text's beginning or conclusion may contain the major theme. To determine whether a passage or paragraph's opening and closing phrases effectively convey the main concept, ask students to identify them.

Students can pose questions to themselves, such as "What is the author trying to tell me?" or "What is this passage mostly about?" Students are better able to concentrate on the text's main idea rather than becoming mired in specifics when they are encouraged to create their own questions.

Use the Title: A text's title frequently offers crucial hints about its core theme. Before reading, students can use the title to predict the main idea of the text if it is descriptive. Students can review the title after reading to see whether it still accurately reflects what they understood of the key topic.

Emphasis on significant Phrases: Students can underline or highlight significant phrases that seem crucial to the text's overall meaning as they read. As they read the passage, this can assist them in determining its major point. To illustrate the core notion, terms like "important," "main point," or "key reason" are frequently used.

Summarize the Text: Students should attempt to condense a passage into a single statement after reading it. They have probably accurately identified the key concept if they are able to summarize the text's major point in a single, succinct statement.

4.5 Techniques for Finding Corresponding Information

Students must locate the details that support the primary notion when they have identified it. The basic idea is clarified by supporting details, which offer proof, justifications, illustrations, or elaborations. Students can use the following techniques to find supporting details in a passage:

Seek Out Facts and Examples: Frequently, supporting information is offered in the form of facts, illustrations, or justifications. The fundamental idea is strengthened by the additional information or clarification these elements offer. Pupils should focus on any numbers, statistics, or particular examples that are included in the text.

Find Descriptive Words or Phrases: Vibrant descriptions can serve as supporting features in narrative or descriptive passages. Students might search for adverbs or adjectives that clarify the main point or help paint a picture.

Be Aware of Transitions: The use of phrases such as "for example," "in addition," "because," and "as a result" indicates the start of supporting information. It is important to teach students to identify these transitional words as indicators that further details or instances will follow.

Distinguish Between Essential and Extraneous Information: Not every detail is equally significant. Students should be encouraged to differentiate between unnecessary details—which offer more, non-important information—and crucial supporting elements, which directly support the main idea. Students will be better able to determine what actually supports the main idea if they concentrate on the most pertinent information.

Make a Graphic Organizer: Students can more effectively visualize the connection between the primary idea and its supporting elements by using a graphic organizer, such as a web or a main idea/detail chart. Students are encouraged to analyze the material and arrange their ideas logically by using this strategy.

4.6 Typical Difficulties in Recognizing the Main Idea and Specifics

Even though it's a crucial skill, third graders may find it difficult to recognize the primary idea and supporting elements, particularly in lengthy or complex texts. Typical difficulties include the following:

Finding Implied key Ideas: Sometimes the key idea is implied rather than expressed outright. Students must do this by deducing the core notion from the supporting details. By highlighting important information and encouraging students to consider the author's purpose, teachers can help students draw conclusions.

Misunderstanding the primary theme: Students can mistake the text's primary theme for a particular detail or incident. For instance, a student may believe that the primary focus of a paragraph regarding animal migration is on a particular kind of animal rather than the more general principle of migration. By asking students to consider the text as a whole and identify the message that connects the details, teachers can assist their students.

Paying Attention to Non-Essential Details: Students occasionally pay attention to details that are fascinating but unrelated to the primary idea. Instructors should assist students in differentiating between secondary facts that might not directly support the main point and important supporting data.

Difficulty with Complex Texts: Students may find it more difficult to discern the primary idea and specifics of texts as they come across increasingly complex texts in the third grade. More attentive reading and practice may be necessary for texts with several themes, a variety of genres, or abstract notions. By segmenting the text into manageable chunks and providing students with step-by-step guidance, teachers can scaffold education.

4.7 Main Idea and Detail Practice Exercises

Teachers can provide third graders a range of exercises and activities to assist them practice recognizing the main concept and supporting details:

Sorting by key concept and Detail: Give students a list of lines from a paragraph and ask them to group them into three categories: non-supporting details, supporting details, and key concept. Students can better organize their ideas and recognize important facts with the help of this practice.

Key Concept Students should fill out a graphic organizer with slots for many supporting elements and a box for the primary concept. This aids pupils in making a visual connection between the details and the main idea.

Group Discussions: Students can read a text in small groups and then talk with their classmates on the primary theme and any supporting details. Group conversations reinforce the value of cooperation in reading comprehension by assisting students in expressing their knowledge and hearing various points of view.

Writing lines: After reading a passage, have students write a sentence summarizing the primary idea and a few lines outlining the facts that support it. This promotes writing abilities and strengthens the connection between the primary idea and specifics.

Interactive Quizzes: Make games or quizzes in which students must select from a selection of possibilities the primary idea and supporting details. An entertaining and interesting method of evaluating comprehension is through interactive tests.

Chapter 5: Inference and Conclusion-Making

The capacity to infer and draw conclusions is one of the main skills evaluated on the Florida FAST Reading Assessment for third graders. These are higher-order thinking abilities that call on pupils to "read between the lines," or go beyond a text's literal interpretation and utilize inference, reasoning, and past knowledge to grasp the underlying meaning. This chapter will examine the definitions of inference and conclusion-drawing, their differences, and methods for assisting third graders in mastering these critical abilities.

5.1 Inferences and Conclusions: What Are They?

Both conclusions and inferences are essential elements of reading comprehension that inspire children to think critically and draw connections that go beyond the text's obvious meaning. They all involve various facets of comprehension, despite their similarities.

Drawing Conclusions: An inference is a well-informed guess or assumption regarding details that aren't explicitly mentioned in the text. It entails drawing an inferred but unstated conclusion by combining the reader's prior knowledge or experiences with hints from the text (such as word choices, character actions, and details). When an author leaves out important elements, leaving the reader to fill in the blanks, inferences are frequently required.

Drawing Conclusions: The process of reaching a decision or judgment based on the data presented in the text is known as drawing a conclusion. In order to comprehend the text's deeper meaning, it entails combining the details and the deductions drawn. Drawing a conclusion entails combining all of the information provided in a paragraph to create an overall assessment, as opposed to drawing an inference, which frequently fills in the blanks.

Although drawing conclusions and inferences are two different processes, they complement one another to help students interact deeply with a material, improving their critical thinking and comprehension. Students that possess these abilities must be able to read beyond the text and decipher what the author suggests, indicates, or omits.

5.2 The Value of Conclusions and Inferences

Making inferences and drawing conclusions is essential to comprehending narratives, educational materials, and even regular conversations. With these abilities, readers can:

Fill in the blanks: Writers frequently omit important information or fail to mention all of the facts in the text. Using context and prior information, inference assists the reader in filling in these gaps.

Recognize characters: Even in cases where motivations, feelings, and actions are not explicitly stated, readers can nevertheless deduce these aspects from inferences. For instance, the reader would assume that a figure is rushing or unprepared for the weather if they are seen sprinting in the rain without an umbrella.

Make inferences: Using the information that has been presented thus far, readers can make inferences about what might occur next in a story. These forecasts keep readers interested and enhance the reading experience.

Go beyond the words: The capacity to infer and draw conclusions aids readers in comprehending the tone, themes, and deeper meanings of the book in addition to the plot and key ideas.

Students are asked to exhibit these abilities in a number of ways throughout the Florida FAST Reading Assessment. Since these abilities are frequently evaluated across all genres and text kinds, students who understand how to draw conclusions and make inferences will perform exceptionally well on the test.

5.3 Interpreting Contextual Hints to Draw Conclusions

Using context clues—the words, phrases, or facts surrounding an unknown word or idea to assist the reader understand its meaning—is an essential part of drawing conclusions. When it comes to assisting pupils in drawing informed conclusions or assumptions about a text, context clues are crucial. Even when not all of the information is provided clearly, students can still make inferences about what is happening by concentrating on the surrounding data.

Contextual cues can be of numerous kinds and aid in drawing conclusions.

Definition or Restatement Hints: Occasionally, a sentence will explain a word or idea's meaning. For instance, "The girl felt melancholy, which is a word that means sad." This lets the reader know right away that "melancholy" denotes "sad."

Synonym Clues: A synonym can be used to help the reader grasp a word that is hard to understand. For example, "When he received the award, he was extremely delighted."

Antonym Hints: Sometimes a word's meaning can be deduced by knowing its opposite. For instance, "The sunny, bright weather was a sharp contrast to the chilly, overcast days that preceded it."

Example Clues: To illustrate a point, a writer may use examples. "Pets, such as dogs, cats, and birds, can provide companionship," for example.

Cause-and-Effect Hints: Sometimes drawing conclusions is aided by knowing what transpired as a result of an occurrence. For instance, "The storm had left the ground damp." In order to keep her feet dry, she put on her boots. The consequence (wearing boots) follows the cause (the damp ground), which aids the reader in understanding the character's motivation.

As they read, students should be taught to use these context clues since it will help them deduce meanings and draw connections between the text.

5.4 Drawing Inferences from Past Experience

When drawing conclusions, a student's prior knowledge—what they already know from earlier experiences or education—can be just as significant as context signals. For example, a student may have prior knowledge about the beach's characteristics if they have been there before. They can utilize that information to deduce details about the text, including the location or the emotions of a character, when they read a paragraph about a beach.

Because they enable pupils to understand a text from their own distinct point of view, inferences derived from past knowledge are potent. This can involve figuring out a character's feelings from the situation or making predictions about the plot based on the usual story structure they've seen in the past.

For instance, based on their past experiences with similar social settings, students may deduce that a youngster who must leave a party early is depressed or dissatisfied. They are able to read the text more deeply because of that prior knowledge.

Students may think critically and interact with the text more completely when they are taught to draw connections between what they have learned and what they have read. This is crucial for reading comprehension on the Florida FAST Reading Assessment.

5.5 Third-Grade Inference and Conclusion Techniques

Teachers can use various ways to assist third-grade pupils in drawing conclusions and inferences. The goal of these techniques is to help students become more adept at critical thinking and using textual evidence to support their arguments.

Pose Inferential Questions: Teachers might help pupils by posing queries that call for deductions. "What do you think the character is feeling based on their actions?" is one example.
"Why, in your opinion, did the author include the weather in this passage?"
"How does the character's nervousness come through?"
Students are prompted by these kinds of inquiries to look beyond the text and make inferences about the author's meaning based on hints.

Think-Alouds: By using think-alouds while reading, teachers can demonstrate how to draw conclusions. A instructor might remark, for instance, "I see that the character is running in the rain without an umbrella. I can assume that the character is either ill-prepared or rushing since it is raining. Teachers assist pupils in understanding the process of drawing conclusions by putting their ideas into words.

Employ Graphic Organizers: To assist students in organizing their thoughts and deconstructing the text, teachers can advise them to utilize graphic organizers. Students can examine how the text's hints lead to their conclusions by using a T-chart, which has one side designated for "text clues" and another for "inference." Students can keep track of their deductions and observe how conclusions are reached with the aid of this visual depiction of the thought process.

Role-playing: Students might act out the feelings or behaviors of characters based on deductions during role-playing exercises that follow the reading of a piece. Students can use role-playing to illustrate that a character in a story is upset if, for example, they are described as shaking their head while staring at the ground.

Inference Cards: Instructors can utilize inference cards with a question on one side and hints from a passage on the other. For instance, a detail on a card might read, "The girl sighed as she looked up at the sky." "What might the girl be feeling, and why?" would be the question on the back of the card. This helps pupils to draw conclusions from the information provided.

5.6 Typical Obstacles to Inference and Conclusion-Making

Young readers may find it difficult to form conclusions and make inferences, especially when texts are abstract or allow for several alternative interpretations. Typical difficulties include the following:

Abstract concept difficulty: Drawing conclusions frequently necessitates comprehending notions that are not explicitly expressed. For instance, goals or feelings are frequently suggested rather being explicitly stated. By giving students tangible examples and demonstrating how to use context clues to deduce these abstract concepts, teachers may help pupils.

There may be more than one correct conclusion drawn from an inference, particularly in narrative or complicated texts. Students who are unclear on which inference is correct may find this irritating. Instructors might offer direction by stressing that some deductions are predicated on the most compelling evidence found in the text.

Ignoring minor facts: When drawing conclusions, minor details frequently carry a lot of weight. Pupils may draw conclusions without thoroughly examining the material or overlook crucial hints. Instructors can help students slow down and pay close attention to all of the material, especially when drawing conclusions.

5.7 Exercises for Drawing Conclusions and Inferences

The Inference Matching Game Give pupils a collection of scenarios along with a list of potential deductions or conclusions. Ask them to match the most likely conclusion or inference to each scenario.

Story Prediction: After reading a story's opening, ask students to make predictions about what will happen next by using the text's hints.

Ask students to make a character inference chart in which they record the character's statements, actions, and any implied feelings or intentions.

Chapter 6: Comprehending Story Structure

One of the most important abilities for third-grade kids getting ready for the Florida FAST Reading Assessment is comprehending the structure of a story. Understanding the main components of a story, including its characters, setting, plot, conflict, climax, and resolution, is known as story structure. Students are better able to evaluate and comprehend the texts they read when they are able to recognize and comprehend these components.

The various elements of story structure, their role in overall comprehension, and methods for assisting third graders in grasping these ideas will all be covered in this chapter. Students who comprehend story structure will be able to conduct more in-depth analyses, forecast outcomes, and draw inferences from the organization of stories.

6.1 Important Story Structure Components

Generally speaking, a story has a fundamental framework with multiple essential components. Students who comprehend these components are better able to deconstruct stories into digestible chunks and comprehend the causes, consequences, and connections between events. The following are the primary elements of tale structure:

Setting: The location and time of a story's events are known as its setting. It contains information about the place, era, climate, and surroundings that contribute to setting the scene for the story's actions. It is essential to comprehend the setting since it gives the characters' choices and actions context.

For instance, "a dark and stormy night" or "an old, creaky house at the edge of town" could be used as setting details in a story about a group of friends visiting a haunted house.

The humans or animals that the story centers on are known as characters. Usually, there are two types of characters: the primary characters, who are at the heart of the story, and the supporting characters, who advance the storyline or offer more background information. Pupils must comprehend the characters' motivations, roles, and interactions with one another.

For instance, the dog may be the primary character in a story about a missing dog, with the owner, the neighbors, and the staff at the animal shelter serving as supporting characters.

storyline: The story's storyline is the series of events that comprise it. The "plot structure," which is frequently broken down into five stages—exposition, rising action, climax, falling action, and resolution—is the pattern that it usually adheres to.

Exposition: This section provides background information, characters, and the setting. It establishes the scene for the remainder of the narrative.

Rising Action: By presenting a conflict or issue that the characters must deal with, the rising action develops the plot. The majority of the action occurs here.

Climax: The story's turning moment is the climax. The main character must choose the most difficult or thrilling choice in this section.

Falling Action: The conflict is resolved by the falling action following the climax. This is the section of the narrative where the tension begins to lessen.

Resolution: This brings the story to a close by settling the conflict and tying up any loose ends.

For instance, the exposition of a fairy tale can present a princess in a realm. As the princess encounters a challenge, such as a dragon, the action intensifies. The princess faces the dragon at the climax, and the falling movement depicts her conquering the obstacle. The princess's rescue and subsequent happy life serve as the resolution.

Conflict: The primary issue or difficulty that the characters deal with is the conflict. It is the tension-maker and plot-driver. Conflicts can be external (a battle with another character or the surroundings) or internal (emotions or ideas).

For instance, the conflict in a narrative about a youngster who wants to win a race could be an external conflict with a competitor runner or it could be his dread of failing.

The story's main idea or underlying message is known as the theme. It is the message the author wishes to convey about society, people, or life. Students are better able to relate to the story's deeper significance when they comprehend the topic.

For instance, the theme of a narrative on teamwork would be "working together is better than working alone."

6.2 The Plot's Organization and Importance

Identifying the plot structure is one of the most crucial components of comprehending tale structure. Students can better divide a story into digestible chunks by using the classic plot structure, which follows a predictable pattern. Because of this framework, readers can comprehend how the story progresses, intensifies, and ends satisfactorily.

Exposition: This section presents the characters, the scene, and the starting point. By establishing the scene for what will happen next, it lays the foundation for the narrative. By posing queries like these, students can get practice recognizing the exposition:

What is the setting of the story?
Who are the primary characters?
What is happening at the start of the story?

Rising Action: The story's primary conflict or issue starts to surface during the rising action. It is the story's longest section, during which the tension and events increase. Pupils should search for hints regarding the main conflict and its evolution. Small issues or challenges that the protagonists encounter along the route can potentially be seen as rising action.

Climax: The story's turning moment is the climax. It is the most tense point and frequently signifies a pivotal choice or action that will decide how the conflict turns out. It is frequently beneficial to ask students:

What aspect of the narrative is the most intense?

How does the protagonist handle the most difficult situation?
Falling Action: Following the climax, the falling action illustrates the fallout and starts to settle the conflict in the narrative. At this point, there is less tension, and students can see how the characters respond to what happens. They can search for:

**What is the outcome of the climax?
In what ways are the issues beginning to be resolved?**

Resolution: By resolving the conflict and concluding the narrative, the resolution offers closure. It could bring a sense of closure and provide answers to unanswered issues. Finding the resolution might provide students a chance to consider the story's lesson and the way the conflict was settled.

6.3 Examining the Role of Characters in the Story

Students must be able to identify the characters' roles in addition to comprehending the plot. The plot revolves around the characters, whose decisions, actions, and development throughout the narrative are crucial to its organization.

Protagonist: Often called the "hero" of the tale, the protagonist is the primary character. They serve as the focal point of the narrative. Usually, the protagonist confronts the issue and attempts to find a solution.

The force or character that stands in opposition to the protagonist is known as the antagonist. This might be a different character, a cast of characters, or simply an idea like doubt or fear.

Characters that help the protagonist or advance the plot are known as supporting characters. They frequently give the narrative complexity and set the scene for the protagonist's actions.

Character Development: Story structure requires an awareness of how characters evolve throughout the narrative. Characters in many stories undergo development or transformation, frequently as a result of overcoming the struggle. Pupils should be urged to consider how the characteristics or actions of the characters change from the start of the story to its conclusion.

6.4 Determining a Story's Theme

The moral or lesson of the narrative is the theme. It frequently has to do with universal ideas like kindness, bravery, or friendship. The theme conveys the story's deeper significance, while the plot tells what happens in the story.

Students can ask themselves the following to determine the theme:

Which lesson does the author hope to impart?
What relevance do the story's events have to actual occurrences or more general ideas?

What do the characters discover at the conclusion of the narrative?
A story about a little girl who conquers her fear of public speaking, for instance, might have the theme "facing your fears leads to personal growth."

6.5 Methods for Teaching Third Graders About Story Structure

It is necessary to break down the ideas into digestible pieces in order to teach third graders about story structure. The following tactics may be useful:

Graphic Organizers: Students can better understand the story structure by using graphic organizers like plot diagrams or story maps. With the help of these organizers, students can more easily comprehend how the tale progresses by dissecting it into its constituent elements: setting, characters, plot, conflict, and theme.

Storytelling: Ask students to recount the tale in their own terms, emphasizing its main points. This aids their comprehension of the events' chronology and interrelationships.

After reading a narrative, have the class complete a chart that lists the many story aspects (setting, characters, plot, etc.). This group exercise promotes conversation while reinforcing the idea of tale structure.

Story Structure Games: Learning may be enjoyable by using games like matching exercises or story structure bingo. Students could, for instance, correlate story events to the appropriate plot structure elements (exposition, rising action, etc.).

Read-Alouds: Take breaks throughout read-aloud sessions to talk about the story's structure at significant junctures. Based on the story's framework, have students guess what might happen next or how the character might respond.

Story Sequencing: Assign pupils to put a series of story events in the right order. Students benefit from this exercise by being able to recognize the events' progression and comprehend the plot's flow.

Chapter 7: Recognizing Textual Elements

When reading in the third grade, kids start to come across a range of text genres and styles. Students need to be aware of the textual characteristics that frequently accompany these texts in order to successfully understand them. Text characteristics are the components that aid in information organization, highlight key ideas, and direct the reader's comprehension. Headings, subheadings, bold text, italics, charts, diagrams, glossaries, indexes, and more are all included. Although they can also be found in narratives, these characteristics are most prevalent in informational writings.

The significance of text characteristics in reading comprehension will be discussed in this chapter, along with the many kinds of text features and methods for third-grade students to comprehend and apply them successfully. Gaining an understanding of text features can help students' reading comprehension throughout their academic careers and is a necessary ability for success on the Florida FAST Reading Assessment.

7.1 Text Features: What Are They?

Text characteristics are elements of a text that make it easier for readers to find information quickly, comprehend the content more readily, and interact with it. They serve as roadmaps to assist readers in navigating and understanding the content.

Among the most prevalent textual characteristics are:

Content is arranged into parts using headings and subheadings, which are titles or subtitles. While subheadings offer more detailed information, headings typically give the reader a general impression of the topic of the section.

An illustration of this would be a science textbook on plants with the heading "Parts of a Plant," with the subheadings "Roots," "Stem," and "Leaves."
Bold font: Important terms or concepts are highlighted with words or phrases in bold font. These are frequently important vocabulary words that the reader should concentrate on or fully comprehend.

For instance, "photosynthesis" and "ecosystem" may be bolded in a textbook to indicate their importance.

Italics: Italics are frequently used to highlight particular words, phrases, or work titles (such as novels or movies). Additionally, they can be applied to term introductions or foreign words.

For instance, the title of a book may be italicized, or a character's ideas may be italicized in a tale.

Captions: These are succinct explanations or descriptions that go with pictures, diagrams, or illustrations. They aid in elucidating the picture and how it relates to the text.

As an illustration, the caption for a photo of a plant might say, "The roots absorb water and nutrients from the soil."

Diagrams and illustrations: These visual tools offer more context or assist make difficult concepts easier to understand. Diagrams frequently demonstrate how things function or how components are related, whereas pictures may give a story more visual appeal.

For instance, a butterfly's life cycle might be depicted in an animal textbook picture, with arrows linking the stages from egg to adult.

Data or information can be represented visually with charts and graphs. Readers may quickly comprehend numerical data, comparisons, and trends with the use of charts and graphs. They frequently come with an explanation or key that explains the symbols being utilized.

For instance, a bar chart could display how many apples were grown in each month of the year.

Glossary: At the conclusion of a book or chapter, a glossary is a list of important terminology and definitions. It aids readers in comprehending technical terms that could be novel or unfamiliar.

For instance, the glossary of a book about ocean life might provide definitions for words like "current," "plankton," and "marine ecosystem."

Index: An index is a collection of subjects or keywords arranged alphabetically with page numbers that directs the reader to the relevant sections of the book. It is frequently found toward the book's conclusion.

For instance, the index will identify the precise pages in a nature book where "birds" are covered if you're looking for information on the subject.

Contents Table: A book's chapters or divisions are listed with their corresponding page numbers in a table of contents, which is often located at the start of the book. It makes it easier for the reader to locate information fast and to know what to expect from the text.

For instance, the table of contents of an animal-themed book would have chapters titled "Mammals," "Reptiles," "Birds," and so forth.
Additional boxes or sections on the page that offer further details on the main text are called sidebars. They frequently add intriguing tidbits, advice, or fascinating information to support the main idea.

For instance, more details about well-known leaders of the era may be included in a sidebar of a Civil War history book.

7.2 How Text Features Help with Understanding

Text characteristics are more than just ornamentation; they aid in students' understanding and memory of the material. Each feature helps with understanding in the following ways:

Headings and Subheadings: These elements help readers understand the material by dividing it into manageable chunks. Before delving into the specifics, students can develop their background knowledge by reading the headlines first and making predictions about what will be covered next.

Bold Print: Words that are bolded aid students in concentrating on key terms and ideas. These are frequently the essential terms that students need to be familiar with in order to comprehend the text's primary ideas. Students should take a moment to consider the meaning of a bolded term, frequently searching the text for its definition or explanation.

Italics: Italics are frequently used to highlight important points or draw the reader's attention to unfamiliar terms. These elements contribute to a deeper comprehension of the text by assisting readers in comprehending the meaning of particular words or concepts.

Students can better grasp how an image supports or enriches the text by using captions, which connect images or visuals to the text. For a more comprehensive grasp of the content, students should pay attention to the captions, which frequently encapsulate the image's main idea.

Diagrams and illustrations: Images are effective tools for comprehending difficult concepts. Students can better understand the relationships between ideas when topics are broken down into smaller, more accessible chunks using diagrams and drawings. Additionally, they assist pupils who might study better visually.

Charts and graphs are tools that visually represent complex data, making it easier to understand. A graph that displays temperature variations over time, for instance, enables pupils to compare values, identify patterns, and formulate hypotheses.

Glossary: A glossary gives students the meanings of words they don't know. This is especially helpful when coming across specialized jargon that could be essential to comprehending the major themes of the book. A glossary improves students' understanding of the subject matter and motivates them to pick up new vocabulary.

Index: Students can swiftly find specific information using an index without having to read the full text. This is particularly useful when conducting research or searching for a specific subject. As students progress through increasingly complex literature, it is crucial that they learn how to use the index.

Table of Contents: Before students begin reading, the table of contents gives them a summary of the text. It facilitates their comprehension of the book's organization, which makes it simpler to navigate and locate information. Efficiency can be improved and time saved by knowing where a particular area is located.

Sidebars: Although they may not be necessary to the main text, sidebars give the reader additional background information, examples, or facts that help them better grasp the subject. They provide more chances for participation and education.

7.3 Instructing Learners on Text Features

Students gain proficiency in navigating and utilizing text features over time. The following techniques will assist third graders in mastering the use of text features in their reading:

Explicit Instruction: Introduce each text feature to the class first. Give books and other materials as examples, describing the function of each feature. Talk about how they can improve their reading comprehension by utilizing these qualities.

Interactive Activities: Design interactive classes that require students to respond to questions using textual elements. Give them a paragraph with a chart, for instance, and ask them to analyze the facts. To assist students in finding the answers, encourage them to make use of headings, captions, and diagrams.

Give students a list of text features to search for in a book or article as part of a text feature scavenger hunt. Request that they locate instances of each feature and describe how it aids in their comprehension of the text. You can do this alone or in groups.

Use visual organizers to assist students in mapping out the ways in which textual characteristics contribute to their comprehension. After reading a passage from a textbook, for instance, assign students to fill out a chart that links the text's main themes with the headings, bold text, and images.

Modeling and Think-Alouds: As you read aloud, show how you comprehend the content by using textual aspects. You may pause and demonstrate, for example, how you use a glossary to comprehend a term that is bolded or how you utilize the table of contents to locate a particular chapter.

Practice with Various Texts: Introduce students to a range of texts that employ various textual elements. Make educational books, articles, and even websites available to them. They will learn how to use multi-featured texts to help them read more effectively the more they engage with them.

Chapter 8: Information Comparison and Contrast

Comparing and contrasting knowledge is one of the most crucial abilities that third-graders acquire. This ability is essential for comprehending the relationships between several kinds of information and for drawing conclusions from a variety of sources. Students can analyze similarities and differences in information, themes, characters, or ideas by using comparison and contrast during reading, which helps them comprehend what they read more deeply.

This chapter will examine the value of comparing and contrasting material, demonstrate its application to students, and provide techniques for improving it in accordance with the Florida FAST Reading Assessment. Students can improve their writing, critical thinking, and reading comprehension by learning how to compare and contrast.

8.1 What Are the Significance of Contrast and Comparison?

Comparing entails looking at two or more things to find commonalities. When comparing, we search for similar qualities or attributes among the objects. Conversely, to contrast is to point out the differences between two or more things. By using comparison and contrast, students are able to identify the similarities and differences between the topics they are studying.

For instance, students may concentrate on the following while contrasting and comparing two animals, such as a dog and a cat:

Comparable similarities include the fact that both are pets, have fur, and are capable of becoming amiable.
Disparities (Contrast): Cats are more independent and frequently need less care, whereas dogs are usually more gregarious and may be taught to obey orders.
Students can better organize their ideas while writing or debating issues and create more meaningful connections between concepts by learning how to compare and contrast.

8.2 What Makes Contrasting and Comparing Vital?

For a number of reasons, the ability to compare and contrast information is crucial in reading and beyond.

Enhances Understanding: Students are prompted to consider the content critically when they compare and contrast, which aids in their deeper comprehension. This ability helps individuals understand the material by encouraging them to deconstruct difficult concepts into digestible chunks.

Enhances Retention: Students can establish links and connections between ideas by recognizing similarities and differences, which facilitates information retention. In topics like physics and history, where students must retain important facts and ideas, this is especially beneficial.

Enhances Critical Thinking: Students' critical thinking abilities are enhanced through comparison and contrast. It compels people to weigh two or more pieces of information, consider their implications, and draw evidence-based conclusions. This is very helpful when making decisions and addressing problems.

Improves Reading Comprehension: Students actively interact with the material as they make comparisons and contrasts. They are now actively connecting the text to what they already know, rather than being passive readers. Overall comprehension is enhanced by this active participation.

Enhances Writing: One of the most important techniques for structuring information in writing is the use of comparison and contrast. Students frequently utilize comparison and contrast when writing essays or reports in order to strengthen their claims or present a fair assessment of various viewpoints.

8.3 How to Contrast and Compare Data

Students need to use specific techniques in order to compare and contrast in an efficient manner. Students can better arrange their ideas and pinpoint important areas of comparison with the aid of these techniques. When comparing and contrasting information, follow these crucial steps:

Choose the Subjects to Compare: Selecting the objects, ideas, or concepts that will be examined is the first stage in the comparison and contrast process. It's critical to choose topics with enough parallels and divergences to warrant meaningful comparison.

For instance, you could contrast two historical events, two animals, or two fictional characters.

Emphasis on Important Features: Students should concentrate on the most pertinent traits to compare and contrast after selecting their subjects. These attributes could include physical characteristics, behaviors, places, time periods, motivations, or any other significant aspect of the participants.

For instance, when students compare two characters, they may concentrate on their roles in the narrative (hero vs. villain), their behaviors (helpful vs. harsh), and their psychological traits (kind vs. selfish).

Search for Parallels and Dissimilarities: Students should start by looking at the similarities (compare) and differences (contrast) after deciding which features to examine. To visually separate and arrange these components, it is useful to make a Venn diagram, T-chart, or other graphic organizer.

Use Textual Evidence: Students should cite certain passages in the text to bolster their observations when comparing and contrasting. For instance, students should support their arguments using exact quotes or examples from the text when contrasting two characters in a novel.

For instance, "The dog and the cat both enjoy playing in the story, but the dog likes to fetch sticks while the cat prefers to play by itself with its toys."

Make inferences: Students should make inferences regarding the connections between the two subjects after recognizing the parallels and discrepancies. What can we learn about the subjects from the comparisons? In what ways do the contrasts enhance our comprehension of the topics?

The dog and the cat are both playful, but the dog's demand for human contact stands in contrast to the cat's independence, for instance.

8.4 Comparing and Contrasting Graphic Organizers

Students can more easily see the parallels and discrepancies between subjects by using graphic organizers. A few kinds of visual organizers that work well for comparison and contrast are as follows:

47

Venn Diagram: An excellent tool for contrast and comparison is a Venn diagram. Two circles overlap, with the left circle standing for one subject and the right for the other. The overlap demonstrates the similarities between the two circles. The regions that don't overlap draw attention to the variations.

For instance, students could add traits like "barks" in the dog's circle and "purrs" in the cat's circle when comparing a dog and a cat. They would include common characteristics, such "has fur," in the overlap.
T-Chart: A T-chart is a straightforward two-column visual organizer that can be used for contrast and comparison. Students can make a side-by-side list of the similarities and differences. When students are studying very simple data, this approach performs effectively.

For instance, while comparing two historical events, a student may make a T-chart in which the similarities (for example, both were significant conflicts) are listed in one column and the contrasts (for example, one was a civil war and the other was an international war) are listed in the other.
Matrix of comparison and contrast: This kind of organizer can be used to compare and contrast three or more subjects because it has more than two columns. Every row denotes a trait, while every column denotes a subject. This format makes a thorough side-by-side comparison possible.

For instance, a matrix that lists characteristics like "appearance," "personality," and "role in the story" can be used to compare several characters in a book.

8.5 Techniques for Reading Comprehension Comparing and Contrasting

The following techniques can assist pupils in honing their reading comprehension skills in comparison and contrast:

Teach Comparison and Contrast Keywords: A comparison or contrast is often indicated by specific words and phrases. For instance, "however," "on the other hand," and "unlike" denote a contrast, but "similarly," "both," and "in the same way" imply a comparison. Students can gain a better understanding of the author's information organization by being taught these keywords.

Encourage kids to read actively by posing queries to them while they read. For instance, "What similarities exist between these two characters?" or "How do these events differ from one another?" This facilitates the identification of topics of comparison and contrast and pushes pupils to think critically about the content.

Group Discussions: Assign students to groups to compare and contrast facts after reading a text. Students' comprehension can be strengthened by peer discussion as they exchange insights and hear other viewpoints.

Ask students to summarize the main ideas in their own words after they have finished contrasting and comparing. They will be better able to remember the material and solidify their comprehension of the parallels and divergences as a result.

Apply to Real-Life Situations: Ask students to compare and contrast aspects of their own lives, such as various pastimes, academic courses, or dietary preferences, to help make comparison and contrast more real. They will be better able to relate the idea to their personal experiences as a result.

Understanding Cause and Effect in Chapter 9

Understanding cause and effect is a crucial reading comprehension skill that aids pupils in examining the connections between acts, events, and outcomes. This ability enables pupils to understand the relationships between events in a text and how one occurrence leads to another. This chapter will examine cause and effect, explain why it is a crucial ability for kids to acquire, and offer methods for improving it in accordance with the Florida FAST Reading Assessment.

9.1 Do Cause and Effect Exist?

Fundamentally, cause and effect describes the connection between an occurrence (the cause) and its outcome (the effect). To put it simply, an effect is what occurs as a result of a cause, and a cause is anything that occurs.

Cause: The rationale for an event.
Effect: The outcome or fallout from that incident.

Students may comprehend how events unfold and how various circumstances contribute to the creation of a story or text by understanding cause and effect. Making sense of stories, nonfiction sections, and even scientific ideas when knowing the reason behind events is crucial requires this ability.

Take the line, "It started raining heavily, so the picnic was canceled," for instance. In this phrase:

The intense rain is to blame.

The picnic has been canceled as a result.
Students can get a deeper knowledge of texts and the world around them by recognizing these cause-and-effect links.

9.2 Why Is It Important to Understand Cause and Effect?

For a number of reasons, the capacity to recognize cause-and-effect linkages is essential.

Enhances Reading Comprehension: Students' comprehension of the connections between various aspects of a story or passage is improved when they are able to identify cause and effect. This makes it easier for them to follow the plot and understand the motivations of the characters.

Enhances Critical Thinking: Students are inspired to consider the order of events critically when they comprehend how one occurrence leads to another. It encourages children to inquire, "What caused this result?" or "Why did this happen?" Analytical abilities are fostered by this way of thinking.

Enhances Writing: By being able to explain why something occurred and what the repercussions were, kids who comprehend cause and effect are better able to write. For example, students must demonstrate how one action results in an outcome while writing persuasively.

Helps Solve Problems: Solving problems requires an understanding of cause-and-effect linkages. Students can create solutions when they are able to pinpoint the underlying causes of issues. This is not merely an academic skill; it is a vital life skill.

Enhances Retention: Students are better able to recall and retain information when they comprehend the reason behind an event. Students who employ cause-and-effect thinking are better able to arrange their ideas and draw logical conclusions from them.

9.3 Determining Textual Cause and Effect

Students must be able to identify certain clues and patterns in the text in order to comprehend cause and effect when reading. The following are some essential methods for recognizing these connections:

Seek Out Signal Words: A lot of texts contain particular words or phrases that indicate cause and effect. A cause-and-effect relationship is frequently indicated by words like because, so, thus, due to, and as a result.

For instance: "He didn't study for the test, so he failed."

Examine the Order of Events: Students who comprehend the sequence of events in narratives are better able to comprehend the reasons and consequences. By observing the order of events, one can determine that the cause will frequently occur before the consequence in time.

For instance: "Everyone was awakened by the sound of the alarm. They consequently got out of bed on schedule.
Ask "Why?" and "What Happened?" Ask yourself, "What happened?" as you read a passage. (This is frequently the result) and "What caused this to occur?" This is the reason. Students can better understand the connections between events by using this straightforward inquiry strategy.

Seek Out Patterns of Behavior: Characters' actions or behaviors might occasionally hint at causes and effects without being mentioned directly. Students can deduce what might have led to a specific conclusion by examining a character's actions or choices.

For instance: "Samantha didn't bring her umbrella, and as a result, she got soaked in the rain."

Take Note of the Text Structure: Cause and effect can be discussed in nonfiction works in paragraphs or sections that describe how one event causes another. Students are better able to recognize these relationships when they comprehend the text's structure.

9.4 Cause and Effect in Various Text Types

Both narrative and informational texts contain cause-and-effect linkages, although they may be portrayed differently:

In Narrative Texts (Stories): The plot of stories is frequently propelled by cause-and-effect linkages. Students must comprehend how one occurrence leads to another because characters' choices, actions, and circumstances have repercussions.

Example: The cause (not studying) leads to the consequence (failing the test) in a story about a character who forgets to study for an exam.
In Nonfiction Informational Texts: Cause and effect is commonly employed in nonfiction works to illustrate how one event influences another or to explain why events occurred. Students are better able to understand the text's basic idea and goal when they comprehend this relationship.

For instance: "Because the forest was not properly maintained, a wildfire spread quickly and caused significant damage."
In Science Texts: A key idea in science that explains natural processes and occurrences is cause and effect. Students can have a better knowledge of how the world functions by comprehending the reasons behind these occurrences.

For instance: "The heat from the sun causes the water in oceans and lakes to evaporate, which leads to the formation of clouds."

9.5 Understanding Cause and Effect with Graphic Organizers

A useful tool for arranging cause-and-effect links visually is a graphic organizer. Some popular visual organizers for teaching cause and effect are listed below:

A straightforward chart with two columns—one for causes and one for effects—is called a cause-and-effect chart. Pupils are able to enumerate several causes and the consequences that follow. This organizer makes the connections between events more clear.

For instance:

Cause: The intense downpour began.
The result was flooded highways.
Chain of Events: A chain of events diagram illustrates the relationship between each event in a series. This is helpful for comprehending how one occurrence influences other ones.

For instance:

Cause: There was a lot of wind.
The tree toppled as a result.
The route was obstructed by the tree.
Fishbone Diagram: This organizer shows the causes of a single effect graphically. On the "fish," the effect is positioned at the head, while the causes are positioned along the "bones."

An illustration of a fishbone diagram might place "failure" at the head of a story about a character's failure, with the bones listing reasons such as "bad decisions," "lack of preparation," and "procrastination."

9.6 Using Real-World Examples to Practice Cause and Effect

Students should be encouraged to try using this skill in real-world situations in order to reinforce cause-and-effect links. Here are some practice techniques:

Connect to Personal Experiences: Inquire about instances in students' personal lives where a cause-and-effect relationship was evident. "What happens if you forget your homework at home?" is one example. The reason (forgetting the homework) and the impact (missing out on class participation) can then be explained by the students.

Examine Everyday Circumstances: Cause and effect are present in every facet of life. Students should be encouraged to think critically about commonplace events, such as the weather, schoolwork, or family gatherings. "Why do plants grow in sunlight?" or "What happens if you forget to set an alarm?"

Talk about Historical Events: Assist pupils in comprehending how historical cause and effect operate. Talk about historical occurrences, such as the reasons for the American Revolution or the wars of particular nations. Students should be asked to determine the reasons and consequences of these occurrences.

9.7 Typical Obstacles to Cause and Effect Understanding

Even while cause and effect is a crucial skill, some children could have trouble comprehending or recognizing these connections. Typical challenges consist of:

Having Trouble Telling the Difference Between Cause and Effect: Students may occasionally mix up cause and effect, particularly if the text does not make this distinction explicit. Teachers can assist by reiterating the notion that the "reason something happens" is the cause, and the "result" is the effect.

Missing Implied Causes and Effects: The cause-and-effect link may not always be explicitly indicated in texts. It is important to teach students to search the text for hints that indicate the reason behind events.

Ignoring Multiple Causes: There are multiple causes for some events. It is important to educate students that complex situations can have several aspects influencing the final result.

Chapter 10: Text Summarization

One of the most crucial reading comprehension abilities a pupil can acquire is summarizing. Students must summarize material from a text and then articulate the key points in their own terms. Effective summarization is essential for students to show that they understand the material, identify important ideas, and communicate information succinctly and clearly on the Florida FAST Reading Assessment. The process of summarizing texts, its significance, and methods for assisting third-grade children in completing summary assignments will all be covered in this chapter.

10.1 Summarizing: What Is It?

The ability to distill a lengthy text into a more manageable chunk while keeping the essential points is known as summarizing. When students summarize, they must highlight the key ideas and omit extraneous details, concentrating only on the most crucial information.

The synopsis is:

Concise: The original material should be longer than a summary.
Accurate: No crucial information should be left out, and the essential elements must be kept.
Clear: The reader should be able to understand a summary with ease.
Take the following paragraph, for instance: "To buy apples, Samantha went to the store. The red apples appeared fresh, so she picked them. She went home and placed her apples in the refrigerator after paying for them.

"Samantha bought fresh red apples at the store and put them in the refrigerator" could be a decent way to sum up this paragraph.

The essential actions—purchasing apples, selecting red apples, and storing them in the refrigerator—are kept in the summary, but unnecessary information—like the fact that she paid for them—is omitted.

10.2 What Makes Summarizing Vital?

A key component of reading comprehension, summarizing offers numerous significant advantages.

Enhances Comprehension: Students are compelled to actively interact with the text and digest the material they have read when they summarize. As a result, the information is better understood and retained.

Promotes Critical Thinking: Students must discern between the primary ideas and illustrative details when summarizing. This helps children better examine the material and comprehend the connections between ideas because it calls for critical thinking and judgment.

Enhances Writing Ability: Students' writing abilities are enhanced by summarizing. Writing essays, reports, and other academic assignments requires the ability to communicate ideas clearly and concisely, which they acquire.

Test-Preparation: Students may be asked to summarize a passage on tests such as the Florida FAST Reading Assessment. Students can perform better on these assessments and show that they understand the literature by being able to describe it well.

Encourages Memory and Retention: By asking students to recollect the key details of a text, summarizing helps them remember what they have learnt. Over time, this facilitates pupils' retention of important ideas.

10.3 Essential Components of an Effective Synopsis

In order to properly summarize, students need concentrate on three key components:

Main Ideas: The text's primary concept is its main point or message. The author wants the reader to comprehend it. Students should highlight the key points and rephrase them in their own terms while summarizing.

The facts, illustrations, or justifications that serve to elucidate or elaborate on the primary idea are known as supporting details. Students should choose the most significant supporting details that aid in elucidating the primary ideas, even though they are not required to include all of them in their summary.

Removal of Superfluous Information: A good summary omits any information that is not essential to comprehending the text as a whole, such as little details, examples, or descriptive language. It merely highlights the most important details.

10.4 Methods for Text Summarization

To guarantee that students capture the most important information, summarizing calls for a methodical approach. A straightforward procedure for summarizing any text is described in the stages below:

Read the Text Carefully: Students need to read the text carefully before attempting to summarize. Before distilling the text into a summary, it is crucial to comprehend it in its totality.

Determine the Main Idea: Students should determine the primary theme or idea after reading the book. "What is the author trying to convey?" is a question to ask. Although the introduction or conclusion usually contains the primary point, students should take care to study the entire piece in order to properly comprehend the material.

Emphasize Key Points: Students should underline or highlight the most crucial passages as they read; these will be the primary concepts and crucial information that should be covered in the summary.

Remove Extraneous Details: After determining the primary points, students should cut out any extraneous details or information that doesn't support the core theme. This could include any repetitious material, additional instances, or brief descriptions.

Rewrite the Main Ideas in Your Own Words: Students should rewrite the text in their own words after determining what is most significant. This entails condensing and simplifying the primary concepts and illustrative elements.

Verify Clarity and Accuracy: After writing a summary, students should go over it to ensure that it appropriately captures the essential ideas of the source material. The summary need to be unambiguous and simple to comprehend, devoid of any further details or subjective viewpoints.

Students should make any necessary revisions to the summary to make sure it is clear, accurate, and succinct. Generally speaking, a summary should be around one-third of the length of the original text.

10.5 Techniques for Summarizing Instruction

Teachers can employ the following techniques to assist third-graders in developing their summarizing skills:

Model the Process: Instructors ought to demonstrate how to condense a text. Students can learn how to pinpoint the core concept, emphasize important details, and rework the text succinctly by going through the processes together.

Employ Graphic Organizers: Students can more effectively arrange the primary concepts and illustrative aspects of a text by using graphic organizers such as Venn diagrams, story maps, and summary charts. By using these tools, students can divide the text into digestible sections, which facilitates the process of writing a summary.

Practice with Short Texts: Teachers should begin by practicing summarizing brief passages in order to gain confidence. Students can go to lengthier and more complicated materials as they gain confidence in summarizing.

Employ High-Interest materials: Make use of materials that pique students' interests in order to keep them interested and make summarizing fun. Stories concerning animals, sports, or subjects that are popular with third graders may fall under this category. Students are more likely to participate in the summary process when they are engaged with the material.

The "Somebody, Wanted, But, So" strategy should be taught. A straightforward summary technique that assists students in distilling a document into four essential elements:

Someone: Who is the subject of the tale?

Desired: What was the character in need of or desiring?

However, what issue or challenge did the character encounter?
So, what was the outcome?
For pupils, this method offers a methodical approach that streamlines the procedure.

Peer Summarizing: Assign students to pairs and ask them to collaborate in summarizing a text. While the other student makes sure the summary is clear and accurate, one student can summarize out loud. The summarizing procedure is strengthened by this peer review.

Strengthen Encouraging students to paraphrase is crucial for effective summarization because it allows them to express knowledge in their own terms. In addition to making the summary more succinct, paraphrasing aids in students' internalization of the material.

10.6 Typical Summarizing Difficulties

Many kids find summarizing difficult, particularly those in the third grade. When summarizing, students frequently encounter the following difficulties:

Paying Too Much Attention to Small Details: Students may find it difficult to discern between the primary idea and supporting details, frequently concentrating excessively on details that are not crucial to the summary.

Over-Summarizing: In an effort to condense the material, pupils occasionally omit too much information. This may lead to a summary that is ambiguous or lacking information.

Students who struggle with paraphrasing must comprehend the source material and rephrase it in their own terms. Some students might find this difficult, which could result in summaries that are overly identical to the source material or that include an excessive amount of direct quotation.

Information Organization: Students may struggle to arrange their ideas and knowledge logically. For this challenge, formal methods such as "Somebody, Wanted, But, So" and graphic organizers can be helpful.

Lack of content Understanding: Students who do not fully comprehend the content find it difficult to summarize. Before summarizing and making sure students understand the content, teachers might assist by having a discussion about the text.

10.7 Using the Florida FAST Reading Assessment to Summarize

Students may be asked to summarize a passage or a section of a passage as part of the Florida FAST Reading Assessment. In this situation, summarizing calls on pupils to show that they comprehend the material and can distill it into a manageable format.

Students should understand that the FAST test will evaluate their ability to pinpoint the text's main concepts and weed out extraneous details. Students can better prepare for this portion of the test by practicing summarization.

Chapter 11: Examining Personas and Their Qualities

Analyzing characters and their characteristics is one of the most important reading comprehension skills that children may acquire. This ability increases their comprehension of the story by assisting them in comprehending the personalities, actions, and motivations of the characters in a text. Students can determine how characters affect the plot, interact with one another, and change as the novel progresses by examining the characters. Analyzing characters and their characteristics is essential for responding to questions about the book and proving a thorough comprehension of the subject matter in the context of the Florida FAST Reading Assessment.

The technique of character analysis, the significance of character analysis for reading comprehension, the essential characteristics of characters to examine, and successful teaching methods for character analysis in texts will all be covered in this chapter.

11.1 Character analysis: what is it?

Analyzing characters in a story entails looking at their characteristics, actions, and motivations. Students should think about the motivations behind the character's acts in addition to the actions themselves when examining them. This entails investigating elements like:

Personality attributes that characterize a person are known as character traits.
Character motives are the explanations for a character's actions.
Character development is the process by which a character evolves or develops over time.
Character interactions: The ways in which characters interact and impact one another.
Students can gain a deeper understanding of a character's role in the story, how they contribute to the storyline, and what lessons they can learn from their experiences by using character analysis.

11.2 The Significance of Character Analysis
Character analysis is crucial for a number of reasons:

Enhances Text Understanding: Students learn more about the story as a whole by examining the characteristics, intentions, and deeds of a character. They start to notice how the character's choices and disposition affect the plot's developments.

Enhances Empathy: Students' empathy is increased when they comprehend the motivations and challenges of a character. It enables them to value diverse viewpoints and comprehend the difficulties that other people encounter.

Enhances Critical Thinking: Students are encouraged to think critically about a text by analyzing characters. "Why did the character make that decision?" is one of the questions they need to ask. such as "How does the character's personality influence the story?" Students that think like this are better able to analyze a variety of texts.

Assessment Preparation: Students may be required to evaluate characters, pinpoint their characteristics, and describe how these characteristics impact the narrative on the Florida FAST Reading Assessment. Students can do better on these kinds of problems by honing their character analysis skills.

Enhances Writing Skills: Character analysis aids pupils in becoming better writers. It pushes them to back up their arguments with textual evidence, which strengthens the argument and organizes their analysis.

11.3 Crucial Personal Qualities to Examine

Although there are many distinct character traits that can be examined, some are especially crucial for assisting students in comprehending the function and growth of a character within the narrative. Among the essential characteristics to examine are:

Physical attributes: These comprise the character's height, eye and hair colors, attire, and other external features. Although a character's physical characteristics do not always constitute their personality, they can provide significant hints about how they see themselves or are viewed by others.

For instance, a character who is described as "tall and imposing" may be seen as powerful or commanding, whereas a character who is described as "small and timid" may be seen as weak or bashful.

The fundamental characteristics that comprise a character's personality are known as personality traits. A person's kindness, selfishness, honesty, bravery, and arrogance are examples of personality qualities. These characteristics are frequently made clear by the character's behavior, ideas, and social interactions.

Example: Characteristics of compassion and selflessness are displayed by someone who is constantly giving, even when it is difficult.

Characters' feelings and emotional expressions are reflected in their emotional qualities. For instance, a character may be joyful, depressed, furious, or nervous. These characteristics can also show how a character responds to various circumstances and difficulties.

For instance, a someone who loses their temper easily over little issues could be characterized as "hot-tempered" or "irritable."

Moral Characteristics: These characteristics pertain to a person's ethics, values, and sense of right and wrong. Strong moral characters might act in ways that are selfish, dishonest, or damaging to others, whereas weak moral characters might make choices that are in line with what is deemed "good."

Example: A character exhibits the moral qualities of loyalty and integrity when they decide to assist a friend in need despite the difficulty of doing so.

Behavioral Traits: These characteristics explain a character's actions in various contexts. These characteristics, which include diligence, laziness, caution, recklessness, and curiosity, can be either positive or negative.

Example: While a character who gives up quickly could be viewed as lacking resolve, a character who works persistently toward a goal exhibits perseverance.

Motivations: The reasons behind a character's choices and behaviors are referred to as their motivation. Why does a character act in a particular manner? Are they driven by ambition, fear, love, or another emotion? Students can more accurately predict how a character will respond to various events in the story when they have a better understanding of the character's motivation.

For instance, a character driven by a desire to keep their family secure may choose to put safety before their own wants.

11.4 Character Analysis Techniques

Character analysis might be difficult, but students can gain a deep comprehension of each character's function and importance by using a methodical approach. Students can properly examine characteristics by following these steps:

Examine the Character's Behavior: One of the most straightforward methods to determine a character's personality is to observe their behavior. Which decisions is the character making? How do they act in various contexts? Are their motives and principles reflected in their actions?

For instance, it indicates that a character is unselfish and caring if they consistently assist people in need.

Examine What the Character Says: Another important way to learn about a character is through dialogue. Take note of the character's speech patterns: is it confident, submissive, angry, or reflective? What does their speech tell us about their mental health and interpersonal relationships?

For instance, a character may be viewed as considerate and sympathetic if they regularly express kindness or provide an apology for their errors.

Analyze the Character's Relationships with Other Characters: What is the treatment of the character by other characters? Are they avoided, feared, or respected? A character's characteristics can be inferred by the way other characters react to them.

For instance, it may indicate that a character is intelligent or reliable if other characters consistently ask them for counsel.

Examine the character's inner conflicts: A character's inner difficulties or struggles can show who they really are. What difficulties or problems do they encounter? How do they handle challenges? Do their experiences cause them to develop or change?

For instance, a character who conquers their fear of public speaking exhibits bravery and personal development.

Examine the Characters' Interactions: Characters' interactions with other characters frequently reveal aspects of their personalities. Does the character push people away or does they develop strong relationships with others? Are they followers or leaders?

Example: While a character who isolates themselves may exhibit introverted or depressed tendencies, a character who is constantly surrounded by friends and loved ones may be perceived as gregarious and kind.

11.5 Methods for Character Analysis Instruction

Learning to examine characters can be a difficult but worthwhile endeavor for third-graders. Teachers might employ the following techniques to assist students in honing their character analysis abilities:

Students should make character maps that emphasize the salient features of each character. Physical characteristics, psychological traits, behaviors, motivations, and relationships can all have their own parts on the map. Students can better arrange their ideas and understand the connections between various facets of the character with the use of this graphic aid.

Employ Graphic Organizers: Students can compare characters, contrast their characteristics, and examine how they evolve throughout the narrative with the aid of graphic organizers such as Venn diagrams or T-charts. Students can better understand connections and relationships with the help of this graphic tool.

Character Journals: Assign students to write in a diary or journal from the viewpoint of a fictional character. Students can consider the character's motivations, thoughts, feelings, and behaviors in each entry. Students have a deeper comprehension of the character's inner life as a result.

Character Role-Playing: Assign pupils to play various characters in scenarios from the literature. Students are better able to comprehend the character's motivations, thoughts, and behaviors as a result of their active engagement.

Pose Guiding Questions: To assist students in character analysis, teachers might pose guiding questions. For instance:

What needs or desires do you believe this character has?

What is this character's response to difficulties?
How is this character perceived by other characters?
In what ways does this character evolve during the narrative?

Chapter 12: Figurative Language Interpretation

A potent technique for expressing meaning beyond the literal interpretation of words is figurative language, which is employed in poetry, fiction, and ordinary speech. It enables authors to convey concepts in imaginative, colorful ways that capture the reader's attention. Gaining a thorough knowledge of texts requires that students comprehend metaphorical language. Understanding figurative language is essential for responding to questions on the Florida FAST Reading Assessment that call for analyzing figurative phrases and their effects on the text.

This chapter will cover the various forms of figurative language, its significance, how it enriches literature, and methods for instructing pupils in its interpretation.

12.1 Figurative Language: What Is It?

The use of words and idioms that depart from their literal meaning in order to express a more profound, symbolic, or creative notion is known as figurative language. Figurative language is used by authors to arouse feelings, conjure mental images for the reader, and enhance the readability of their work. It is intended to strengthen the text's overall meaning rather than to be interpreted literally.

The following are some typical examples of metaphorical language:

Personification with Simile Metaphor
Exaggeration
Onomatopoeia
Alliteration Phrases
Symbols
It is essential for pupils to comprehend figurative language since it enhances their reading comprehension and helps them decipher the words' underlying meanings.

12.2 The Significance of Comprehending Figurative Language Enhances Comprehension: Figurative language gives texts additional levels of meaning. Students can better understand the author's goal and the book's emotional or thematic overtones when they are able to analyze the text through the use of figurative language.

Improves Interpretation: Figurative language is frequently used in works, particularly poetry, to evoke a certain feeling or express nuanced emotions. For instance, the phrase "The stars danced in the sky" employs a metaphor to help readers visualize the stars' beauty and motion, conjuring up a strong mental image.

Boosts Vocabulary: Students' vocabulary grows when they are exposed to metaphorical language. They become more linguistically flexible and creative as a result of learning new idioms, phrases, and interpretations.

Enhances Analytical Skills: Students must consider word usage critically in order to comprehend figurative language. This enhances their capacity to evaluate how particular linguistic choices add to the text's meaning, recognize important themes, and analyze texts.

Exam Preparation: Students are likely to face questions pertaining to figurative language on tests such as the Florida FAST Reading Assessment. Students will be better able to respond to these questions if they comprehend the role of figurative phrases and how they affect the text.

12.3 Figurative Language Types

Figurative language comes in a variety of forms, each with a distinct function in writing. The most prevalent types of figurative language that students will come across in texts are examined here.

A simile A simile compares two dissimilar items by using the terms "like" or "as." Similes are frequently employed to evoke strong feelings in readers and give them a fresh perspective on a subject.

For instance: "Her smile was as bright as the sun."

Explanation: This simile implies that the character's smile was warm and dazzling by comparing its brilliance to the sun.
Similar to a metaphor, a metaphor compares two unlike things without the use of "like" or "as." Rather, a metaphor asserts that one thing is another, frequently implying a more profound relationship or similarity.

For instance, "Time is a thief."
Explanation: This metaphor highlights how ephemeral time can be by implying that it robs us of moments in our life.
Personification Personification is the process of endowing inanimate objects or abstract ideas with human traits or attributes. The reader may find an item, concept, or animal more relatable as a result.

For instance: "The wind whispered through the trees."
Justification: By implying that the wind is capable of whispering, a human behavior, the wind is personified. The natural world appears more dynamic and alive as a result.
Exaggeration An exaggerated statement or claim that is not intended to be taken literally is called hyperbole. It is frequently employed to produce a dramatic effect or for emphasis.

"I've told you a million times," for instance.

Explanation: The hyperbole highlights how often the speaker has repeated herself, even though they haven't actually told the individual a million times.
Onomatopoeia Words that mimic the natural sounds connected to the things or activities they describe are known as onomatopoeia. These words enable readers to see the actions in the text and hear the sounds.

For instance, "The bees buzzed in the garden."
Explanation: "Buzzed" mimics the sound of buzzing, adding richness to the sentence's sensory elements.
Alliteration The recurrence of the same consonant sound at the start of adjacent or closely related words is known as alliteration. It is frequently employed for rhythm and emphasis.

For instance: "The sly snake slithered silently."

Justification: The "s" sound is repeated, which highlights the snake's cunning motions and produces a rhythmic impression.
Idioms Idioms are expressions in which the overall meaning differs from the meanings of the individual words. Idioms can be difficult to grasp if one is unfamiliar with the phrase and are frequently culturally specific.

"It's raining cats and dogs," for instance.

Justification: This expression does not imply that actual cats and dogs are appearing out of thin air. Rather, it indicates that it is pouring rain.
Symbols The use of an item, person, or occasion to symbolize something other than its literal meaning is known as symbolism. Deeper meanings that connect to more general themes are frequently associated with symbols.

For instance, a dove frequently represents peace.
Justification: The dove symbolizes peace since it is typically connected to messages of harmony and serenity.

12.4 How Texts Are Improved by Figurative Language

Figurative language contributes significantly to a text's enrichment. It can assist communicate difficult feelings or concepts, set the tone, and enhance the meaning of a story. Figurative language enriches texts in the following ways:

Produces Vibrant Imagery: Readers are able to conjure vivid images in their minds that surpass the text's precise explanations thanks to figurative language. This makes the content more vivid and captivating, which improves the reader's experience.

For instance: "The golden sunlight spilled over the horizon."
Justification: This metaphor conjures up the warmth and beauty of the sun's light spreading across the sky.
Conveys Complex Emotions: Authors can convey abstract ideas or complex emotions in an accessible and powerful way by using figurative language. This enables readers to relate to the text on an emotional level.

For instance: "His heart was a locked box, hiding all his deepest secrets."
Interpretation: This metaphor implies that the character is protecting and concealing his emotions by comparing them to a closed box.
Sets Mood and Tone: Figurative language can be used to set the tone (the author's attitude toward the subject) and mood (the text's emotional ambiance).

For instance: "The storm raged with fury, crashing against the shore."

Justification: The storm's metaphor of "raging with fury" emphasizes the strength and chaos of nature while evoking a dramatic and passionate atmosphere.

Draws Focus on Important Themes: Figurative language can draw attention to a text's main ideas. For instance, a recurrent metaphor or symbol could draw attention to a main concept, like love or freedom.

For instance, Maya Angelou's "I Know Why the Caged Bird Sings" uses the image of a "caged bird" repeatedly to represent oppression and the desire for release.

Enhances the Language: To enhance the interest and engagement of their writing, authors employ figurative language. Figurative language entices readers to interact with the text more fully by stimulating their senses.

For instance: "The laughter echoed like a sweet melody through the halls."
Explanation: By equating laughter with a melody, this simile elevates the sound and makes it appear more welcoming.

12.5 Methods for Figurative Language Instruction

Students may find it difficult to understand figurative language, particularly when they are initially introduced to it. The following list of techniques can assist students in comprehending and interpreting figurative language more effectively:

Gradually Introduce Figurative Language: Begin by presenting one kind of figurative language at a time. Show students how figurative language functions using examples from well-known books, then ask them to recognize it in context.

Employ Visual Aids: Students can better comprehend the meanings of figurative idioms by using visual aids such as charts, pictures, and graphic organizers. A chart might, for instance, illustrate the distinction between literal and metaphorical interpretations, providing examples for each.

Give Context: Always give context while teaching figurative language. Assist students in correctly interpreting the meaning of figurative expressions by helping them comprehend the context in which they are employed.

Promote Creative Expression: Assign pupils to provide original figurative language examples. This enables students to gain a better understanding of how it works and practice using it in a controlled environment.

Group Activities: Promote group projects in which students examine works that use figurative language together. This encourages group learning and aids in their comprehension improvement.

Use multimedia to engage students and make learning more fun. Examples of this include interactive games, songs, and videos that use figurative language.

Teach Figurative Language in Context: Explain figurative language in the context of a passage or poem rather than just definitions. Talk about how the text's overall meaning is influenced by the metaphorical language.

Reinforce with Practice: Provide pupils with several chances to practice recognizing and deciphering metaphorical language. Utilize assignments, tests, and worksheets to help students understand the material.

Chapter 13: Examining Texts with Information

Students need to be able to read informational literature, particularly when it comes to standardized tests like the Florida FAST Reading Assessment. Informational texts are created to educate, explain, describe, or teach the reader about a certain subject, as opposed to narrative texts, which tell stories. These writings appear in a variety of areas, such as science and social studies, and they are also present in everyday life in the form of news items, ads, and directions. The characteristics of informational texts, reading and comprehension techniques, and advice for efficiently evaluating these books to enhance reading performance will all be covered in this chapter.

13.1 Informational Texts: What Are They?

One kind of non-fiction writing that seeks to inform the reader on a certain subject is an informational text. Informational writings include facts, explanations, or instructions that improve the reader's knowledge or comprehension of real-world topics, in contrast to fictional texts, which are meant to entertain. Textbooks, encyclopedias, newspaper articles, brochures, biographies, scientific reports, and instructional manuals are a few examples of informational texts.

Important traits of informational texts consist of:

The main objective is to describe, clarify, or educate. Instead of entertaining or telling a story, the author concentrates on giving accurate information.
Structure: To help arrange the material and make it easier for the reader to understand, these texts frequently include headings, subheadings, bullet points, charts, graphs, and other visual components.
Content: The material offers facts backed up by study or evidence, descriptions of procedures or events, and real-world expertise.
Language: Informational writings frequently use formal, straightforward, and unambiguous language. Usually, it doesn't use sentimental or exaggerated words.

13.2 Informational Text Types

Students may come across a variety of informational text kinds in their daily and academic reading. The following are the most typical categories:

Texts that provide explanations Expository texts provide a detailed explanation or description of a subject. They seek to make difficult concepts or procedures simpler for readers to comprehend. News stories, history textbooks, and scientific books are a few examples.

An example would be a textbook that explains the process of photosynthesis.
Key Feature: Offers thorough justifications backed by data.
Texts on Procedures To assist the reader in finishing a task or comprehending how something operates, procedural texts offer detailed instructions or directions. Cookbooks, DIY guides, and instruction manuals frequently contain them.

For instance, a pancake recipe.

The main characteristic is that it includes a series of actions or numbered stages.

Texts That Convince The goal of persuasive informational writings is to persuade the reader to embrace a given viewpoint or follow a particular course of action. They frequently appear in persuasive essays, opinion pieces, and ads.

For instance, a magazine article outlining the advantages of a specific diet.
Key Feature: Convinces the reader with logic and proof.
Texts that describe Detailed descriptions of a person, place, event, or object are the main goal of descriptive literature. They seek to evoke a mental image of the topic in the reader.

A travel brochure that describes a national park is one example.

Key Feature: Provides a detailed description of the subject using sensory language.
Articles with Information Typically, websites, periodicals, and newspapers publish informative material. They offer accurate knowledge on a certain subject, including recent discoveries, historical facts, or current occurrences.

An article addressing the effects of climate change is one example.
Key Feature: Provides facts, frequently accompanied by expert quotes or statistics.

13.3 Characteristics of Texts with Information

To effectively explore and grasp informational texts, students need to be able to recognize and understand a variety of their features. Key components frequently included in these kinds of literature are listed below:

Subheadings as well as headers

Headings and subheadings serve to highlight the key concepts and divide the material into digestible chunks.
Benefit: They make it easier for readers to navigate the text and spot important themes fast.
Contents Tables

Goal: Offers a synopsis of the main ideas and organization of the book.
Benefit: Gives readers a summary of the content and assists them in finding specific information.
Index

The goal is to provide an alphabetical list of the subjects discussed in the book, accompanied by the page numbers of the relevant sections.
Benefit: Makes it possible for readers to locate particular material in a book or report with ease.
A glossary

Definitions of significant or specialist terms used in the text are provided via a glossary.
Benefit: Assists readers in comprehending jargon or complicated terms.
Labels and Captions

The goal is to give images, charts, and infographics more context or information.
Benefit: Improve comprehension of the images and how they relate to the text.
Diagrams, Graphs, and Charts

Visual depictions of information, procedures, or structures are the goal.
Benefit: Make abstract or numerical material easier for readers to understand.
Lists and Bullet Points

The goal is to arrange data into clear, understandable points.
Benefit: Simplify difficult information and highlight important ideas.
Sidebars

Goal: Provide fascinating facts or supplemental information that is connected to the primary text but not essential to the main argument.
Benefit: Offer more background information or clarification on particular subjects.

13.4 Techniques for Informational Text Reading

Different methods are needed to read narrative texts and factual writings. Since informational writings frequently have a denser and more sophisticated vocabulary, it's critical to approach them using particular techniques. Some useful techniques for reading informational literature are listed below:

A sneak peek at the text Spend a few minutes skimming the content before reading it in its entirety. Examine the captions, headings, subheadings, and any graphics, such as graphs or charts. This will help you discover important subjects and provide you with a summary of the text.

Determine the Goal Recognize the text's purpose. Is the author attempting to depict, convince, or educate the reader? As you read, being aware of the author's intention will help you concentrate on the most important facts.

Emphasize the main points. Underline or highlight significant words, facts, or ideas as you read. Usually, headings, subheadings, or sentences that provide a summary of the material contain these.

Search for Unfamiliar Terms Technical terms are frequently used in informational writings. Make an educated guess using context clues if you come across a word you don't understand, or consult a glossary if one is provided.

Make Notes Jot down significant definitions, facts, or concepts in your own words. This improves your ability to digest and remember the information.

Make Use of Text Features Take note of textual elements such as charts, sidebars, and captions. These features frequently provide important details that will help you grasp the subject matter better.

Provide a summary of the data n After reading, pause to summarize your understanding. This guarantees that you have comprehended the key aspects and serves to strengthen the information.

Make Inquiries Ask yourself questions concerning the content as you read it. What message does the author want to get across? Which examples or proof are offered to bolster their arguments? What connections exist between the text's various sections?

13.5 Examining Texts That Provide Information

Students should concentrate on more in-depth analysis of informational texts after they have mastered the fundamentals of reading. Analyzing a text entails looking at the author's information organization and presentation, argumentation, and the how the text's structure affects the message as a whole.

Examine the Structure Think on the text's organization. Is it problem-and-solution, cause-and-effect, or chronologically organized? Readers can better grasp how the information is arranged and how it advances the text's goal when they are aware of the structure.

Assess the Evidence Examine the evidence that is provided in the text. Does the author offer facts, illustrations, or professional judgments? To what extent is the evidence reliable? Does the author discuss limitations or rebuttals?

Recognize the Author's Opinion The author's viewpoint on a subject is frequently reflected in informative texts. Check to see if the author is biased or providing facts objectively. Does the author try to convince the reader by using strong language or emotive language?

Combine Data Combine the knowledge you have gained from the various textual sections. How do the different components of the text come together to form a coherent explanation or argument? This will aid in your comprehension of the entire material.

Establish Links Think about the connections between the text's content and your prior knowledge. Is it possible to connect the book to other subjects you have studied or to actual occurrences? Creating connections helps put new information into context and improves comprehension.

How to Respond to Multiple-Choice Questions in Chapter 14

The Florida FAST Reading Assessment is one of the many standardized tests that mostly relies on multiple-choice questions (MCQs). They are employed to test a student's critical thinking, problem-solving, and reading comprehension abilities in addition to their comprehension and interpretation of texts. To succeed on these tests, it is crucial to comprehend how to approach and respond to multiple-choice questions. This chapter will cover multiple-choice question answering techniques, typical mistakes to avoid, and how to use the text's context to inform your responses.

14.1 Multiple-Choice Question Structure

A stem (the question or statement), a list of potential solutions (choices), and one right answer are the usual components of multiple-choice questions. Students will be able to handle these questions more skillfully if they comprehend their structure.

Stem: The stem poses the query or issue that requires resolution. It could be a direct inquiry or a statement that needs to be completed by the student.

For instance: "What is the main idea of the passage?"
Options: A range of potential responses make up the choices. There are usually four or five choices: one right response and multiple distractions (partially right or erroneous replies).

Example Selections: A) The primary concept concerns the risks associated with pollution.

B) The significance of recycling is the central theme.
C) The primary concept pertains to various forms of pollution.
D) The impact of pollution on animals is the central theme.
Correct Response: The response that most effectively addresses the stem is the right one. The choice that best captures the passage's primary idea, topic, or details is this one.

Distractors: The wrong answers are distractions. They are not entirely accurate, but they are meant to appear credible. Common misunderstandings, little nuances, or other aspects of the text that could perplex the reader could serve as distractions.

14.2 How to Approach Multiple-Choice Questions

It takes a combination of critical thinking, test-taking techniques, and strong reading comprehension to answer multiple-choice questions. Students can tackle multiple-choice questions more accurately and confidently by using the following strategies:

First, read the question. Carefully read the question before beginning to read the chapter or material. When reading, this will help you concentrate on locating the precise information you require. Knowing ahead of time whether the question relates to a particular detail or the major theme can help you focus your reading.

As an illustration, if the question is, "What is the main theme of the passage?" concentrate on comprehending the theme while reading the passage. If a particular aspect is the subject of the question, focus on the passage's mentions of that detail.
Carefully read the passage. Read the passage carefully after reading the question. The introduction, conclusion, and any important topics that might be connected to the question should all receive particular consideration.
Underline or highlight significant passages as you read, such as the primary idea, crucial details, or words that could help you answer the question.

Advice: Take your time reading the passage. Give it your complete attention, and go over any confusing or difficult passages again if needed.
Seek Out Contextual Hints Use the surrounding sentences' context to help you understand words or phrases that are challenging for you. This can help determine the right response, particularly when dealing with new words.

Remove Clearly Incorrect Responses Examine the response options after reading the passage and the question. Remove any responses that are obviously incorrect. This lowers the number of possibilities and raises the possibility that the right one will be selected. Seek out distractions that:

are either too general or too specific.

Don't respond to the question directly.

Add details or facts that the passage does not support.

For instance, an answer choice that offers a statement of fact rather than an opinion can typically be removed if the question asks about the author's viewpoint on a subject.

Examine the question and answer choices for keywords. Examine the question and response options for terms like "always," "never," "most," and "some." These terms may offer crucial hints about the right response.

"Always" or "Never": A statement is less likely to be true if it employs an absolute phrase like "always" or "never," as the section may contain an exception.
Because they allow for some diversity, statements that use the words "Most" or "Some" are frequently more likely to be true.

Examine Each Option for an Answer Once you have ruled out solutions that are blatantly wrong, carefully consider the options that remain. Consider this:

Is the question well addressed by this response?
Does the passage provide support for this?
Does it fit the passage's perspective or tone?
Answers that don't fully address the question but appear to be partially correct should be avoided.

Respond Using the Text as a Guide, Not Outside Information Answers on standardized tests, such as the Florida FAST Reading Assessment, should only draw from the text's content. Refrain from answering the question with personal beliefs or outside expertise. Even if the answer goes against what you think is true, the one that the text supports is the right one.

14.3 Common Mistakes to Steer Clear of

Students should be mindful of frequent hazards that can result in inaccurate answers while responding to multiple-choice questions. These consist of:

Reading Too Fast It is possible to miss important elements or cause misconceptions if you rush through the passage or the questions. Before choosing an answer, take your time to make sure you comprehend the text and the question.

Thinking Too Much About the Question Making mistakes might result from second-guessing or overanalyzing oneself. After removing obviously wrong answers and carefully weighing the remaining options, stick with your first response until the passage provides evidence to the contrary.

Selecting the Sounding Answer Rather Than the Correct One Although some of the response options might seem reasonable, the passage does not directly support them. Don't pick responses just because they "sound good" or fit your personal beliefs. Always select the response that is supported by particular textual details.

Misunderstanding the Question Students can misunderstand the question itself, particularly if it is written in a confusing manner. Before responding, make sure you understand the question completely. For better understanding, reword it in simpler terms if needed.

Ignoring the question's "Except" or "Not" Words like "except" or "not," which alter the question's meaning, are used in some multiple-choice questions. Make sure to take note of these terms and modify your perspective accordingly.

For instance, the question "Which of the following is NOT a reason the author suggests recycling?" asks you to choose the response that the passage does not support.

14.4 The Elimination Process

The process of elimination is one of the most effective methods for responding to multiple-choice questions. With this approach, the wrong response alternatives are gradually removed until there is just one choice left. Here's how to put this tactic into practice:

Carefully read the question: Prior to examining the possibilities, comprehend the question.

Examine each possible response: Remove any choices that are obviously incorrect.
Reduce the number of options you have: Once the most obvious wrong responses have been ruled out, give the remaining choices additional thought.
Select the most appropriate response: Based on the information in the passage, choose the option that best responds to the question.

14.5 Use Sample Questions to Practice

You must practice answering multiple-choice questions if you want to get better at it. This is an example of a passage-based multiple-choice question. Try answering the question using the techniques that were covered.

Text: "Recently, a team of researchers found a new kind of fish in the ocean's depths. This species survives in total darkness and feeds on bacteria found on the ocean floor, in contrast to other fish that depend on sunshine for sustenance.

What is the primary characteristic of the recently identified fish species?

A) It feeds on sunlight.
B) It inhabits shallow waters that are close to the surface.
C) It consumes microorganisms found deep within the water.
D) Its food comes from other animals.

It consumes germs in the ocean's depths, thus option C is the right response. The passage's assertion that the fish feeds on microorganisms found on the ocean floor and flourishes in darkness provides direct support for this. According to the information in the passage, the other options are not correct.

Chapter 15: Concluding Recap and Exam-Taking Advice

Students should have a well-thought-out plan for both final review and test-taking techniques as they get ready for the Florida FAST Reading Assessment. The test is intended to evaluate a broad variety of reading abilities, including word identification, phonics, and the capacity to comprehend and interpret challenging literature. In order to assist students do their best on the test, this chapter will offer crucial advice on final preparation, including review methods, test-day strategies, and mindset exercises.

15.1 Why a Final Review Is Important

Prior to any test, the last review time is crucial. Students use this time to solidify their comprehension of the content they have been studying and concentrate on reiterating important ideas. Numerous abilities are assessed by the Florida FAST Reading Assessment, and a concentrated review can significantly increase confidence and guarantee material knowledge.

1.1 Schedule Your Review Period n

During the last review stage, efficient time management is crucial. The last days or weeks leading up to the test should ideally be devoted to strengthening the areas in which pupils are least confident. This is how you go about it this time:

Make a timetable: Give each test section a designated time slot. Be sure to divide your study sessions into digestible portions, such as 45-minute blocks interspersed with brief breaks.
Make your weak areas a priority: Concentrate your efforts on the areas that require the greatest development. For instance, spend more time studying the subject if you have trouble comprehending cause-and-effect linkages.
Go over all the important ideas: Don't completely ignore any areas. To make sure everything is still fresh in your mind, it's crucial to quickly review any areas in which you feel secure.

1.2 Work on Sample Questions

It is essential to practice with sample questions after going over the material. Use practice exams that are similar to the Florida FAST Reading Assessment in terms of both format and difficulty. Students can evaluate their progress and become acquainted with the kinds of questions they will face by taking these practice exams.

Simulate test conditions: To enhance your timing and lessen test anxiety, practice responding to questions in a timed setting. This will give you an idea of how long to spend on each question and help you get used to working under pressure.
Examine incorrect responses: Always check over your answers, including the ones you answered correctly, when you are practicing with example questions. For the ones you overlooked, comprehend why the proper response is the right one and why your selection was wrong.

1.3 Make Use of Active Memory

Active recall is an effective study technique. Test your knowledge of the content actively rather than passively reviewing your notes. During your review, try these active recall techniques:

Make flashcards for language, important ideas, and tactics. Write a query or idea on one side and the response or explanation on the other.
Self-testing: Test yourself frequently on important subjects including figuring out the core idea, comprehending cause and effect, and deciphering metaphorical language.
Peer review: Ask a friend or relative to test you on key ideas if at all possible. This will help you strengthen your knowledge and replicate an actual test-taking atmosphere.

15.2 Successful Test-Taking Techniques

Success requires not only going over the material again but also understanding how to approach the test. Students can perform at their highest level under pressure by using efficient test-taking techniques.

2.1 Carefully read the instructions.

Spend some time attentively reading the instructions before starting the test. Errors that may have been readily prevented can result from a failure to understand the instructions. Make sure you know how many questions the test will include, how much time you have, and what to do if you need help.

Time management: Learn the allotted time for each component of the test, if it is timed. Don't spend too much time on any one question, but give each one adequate time.

2.2 First, quickly review the questions.

It can be useful to quickly go over the questions before reading the passage. This enables you to concentrate on the important details and the kind of information you should seek out when reading the paragraph.

Pay attention to the important words: Highlight the terms in the questions that will help you find the most crucial information in the section while you're skimming, such as "main idea," "author's purpose," and "effect on characters." Mentally get ready: You can increase your speed and accuracy by skimming the questions to gain a better knowledge of what to concentrate on when reading.

2.3 Carefully read the passage.

After glancing over the questions, carefully and thoroughly read the passage. Keep an eye out for key information as you read and jot down anything that seems related to the topics you went over.

Emphasize the key points: Underline or highlight important sentences, details, or hints in the reading that might be relevant to the question, if the test permits.
Don't hurry: Although time management is crucial, take your time reading. Before answering the questions, make sure you have a thorough understanding of the reading.

2.4 The Elimination Process

Apply the process of elimination when responding to multiple-choice questions. Eliminating options that are blatantly wrong will improve your odds of selecting the right answer, even if you're not confident about it.

Mark erroneous responses: Mark incorrect answers if you are certain that at least one of the options is wrong. You will have fewer options as a result, which will make it simpler to determine the right response.
Avoid becoming bogged down in a single question: If you have doubts about a response, go on and revisit it at a later time. Answering one question for too long can keep you from answering others that could be simpler.

2.5 Take Your Time

It's crucial to pace yourself during the exam. You risk running out of time for other questions if you spend too much time on one. The following are some methods for pacing:

Establish time limits: Assign a specific amount of time to each segment or set of questions. Take ten to twelve minutes, for instance, to read each passage and respond to questions about it.
If you're stuck on a question and after a reasonable period of time you still can't figure it out, move on to the next one and return to it later.

2.6 Don't Guess at Tough Questions

Even while answering a question is usually preferable to leaving it unanswered, it's crucial to refrain from speculating when you don't know the right response. It could be advisable to skip the question and come back to it later when you have more clarity if you are unable to rule out any possibilities or infer the answer from the material.

15.3 Test-Day Mindset Advice Mental preparation is equally as crucial as academic preparation. Anxious or agitated students are less likely to succeed than those who approach the test with a composed, concentrated attitude. Here are some tips for being upbeat and self-assured throughout the test.

3.1 Remain Upbeat

Positivity can help lower anxiety and increase confidence. Remind yourself that you possess the abilities and know-how to succeed and have faith in your preparation.

Positive affirmations, like "I am well-prepared" or "I will do my best," are a good way to start the day.
Pay attention to the here and now: Instead of worrying about the test as a whole or about previous errors, focus on each question as it comes along.

3.2 Control Your Test Anxiety

Although test anxiety is normal, it doesn't have to be incapacitating. The following techniques can help you cope with stress both before and during the test:

Breathing techniques: To relax, try deep breathing techniques. For four seconds, take a leisurely breath, hold it for four seconds, and then release it for four seconds.
Visualization: Before the test, picture yourself entering the testing facility, at ease, and confidently finishing it.
Thinking positively: When you start to feel nervous, focus on the things you can control, including your preparation and the effort you put into each question.

3.3 Have a Restful Sleep

Make sure you got a decent night's sleep the night before the test. Your brain will be alert and prepared to function at its peak when you get enough sleep. Steer clear of last-minute cramming since it might cause needless tension and exhaustion.

Relaxation: To improve your quality of sleep, do something calming before bed, like reading a book or practicing mindfulness.

15.4 On the Day of the Test

Preparation is essential on exam day. Bring any necessary supplies (such as identification, a pencil, or an eraser), arrive early, and drink plenty of water. To prevent any tension at the last minute, make sure everything is prepared the night before.

Eat a balanced breakfast: A good breakfast will keep you alert and help your brain function properly during the test.
Get there early: Getting there early gives you time to get settled and get ready for the test.

Practice Questions and Answers Explanations Latest Edition

1. Which of the following is the main idea of this passage?

A) The importance of reading books
B) How animals find food
C) Why exercise is good for your body
D) The different types of trees in a forest

Answer: C) Why exercise is good for your body

Explanation: The main idea of the passage focuses on the benefits of physical activity for your health, including strengthening the heart and muscles. While other details may be mentioned, they support this central idea.

---

2. Which word is a synonym for "quick"?

A) Fast
B) Slow
C) Heavy
D) Strong

Answer: A) Fast

Explanation: "Fast" is a synonym for "quick" because both words mean to move at a high speed. Synonyms are words that have the same or nearly the same meaning.

---

3. What is the effect of the storm on the animals in the story?

A) They go to sleep early.
B) They seek shelter in the trees.
C) They get sick from the rain.
D) They stop searching for food.

Answer: B) They seek shelter in the trees.

Explanation: The animals in the story react to the storm by looking for a safe place to stay, which is the shelter in the trees. This is the cause-and-effect relationship in the passage.

4. What is the genre of the following passage? "A boy discovers a hidden treasure in a cave."

A) Biography
B) Mystery
C) Fantasy
D) Adventure

Answer: D) Adventure

Explanation: The story involves a boy discovering treasure, which is a typical plotline for an adventure story. Adventure stories often involve exciting and dangerous quests.

---

5. Which of the following is a text feature that helps readers understand the story?

A) Heading
B) Textbox
C) Title
D) None of the above

Answer: A) Heading

Explanation: Headings help organize the content and give readers a clue about the main topic of a section. Other text features, like a title or textbox, provide additional information, but headings are specifically used for this purpose.

---

6. What is the meaning of the word "brave" as used in this sentence: "The brave knight rode into the dark forest"?

A) Scared
B) Strong
C) Courageous
D) Angry

Answer: C) Courageous

Explanation: "Brave" means showing courage or fearlessness in the face of danger. In this context, it describes the knight's courage as he enters the dark forest.

---

7. Which detail from the story supports the main idea that teamwork is important?

A) The team worked together to build a fort.
B) The characters fought over who would lead.

C) One person carried all the supplies alone.
D) The group agreed to work in silence.

Answer: A) The team worked together to build a fort.

Explanation: This detail illustrates how teamwork was essential in the story. The team cooperated and completed a task by working together, which supports the idea that teamwork is valuable.

---

8. Which of these words is an antonym for "quiet"?

A) Loud
B) Calm
C) Soft
D) Silent

Answer: A) Loud

Explanation: An antonym is a word that has the opposite meaning of another word. "Loud" is the opposite of "quiet."

---

9. What is the main idea of the paragraph? "Bears hibernate during the winter to stay warm and conserve energy."

A) Bears hibernate in the summer.
B) Bears find food in the winter.
C) Bears sleep in the winter.
D) Bears like cold weather.

Answer: C) Bears sleep in the winter.

Explanation: The main idea of the paragraph is that bears sleep during winter to conserve energy. Other details support this central concept, but this sentence sums it up.

---

10. What is the setting of the story? "The characters were walking along the beach on a bright, sunny day."

A) In the forest
B) At the park
C) At the beach
D) In a busy city

Answer: C) At the beach

Explanation: The setting is where and when the story takes place. The passage mentions a beach, making it the setting.

---

11. What is the effect of the character's choice to ignore the advice given by others?

A) They win the race.
B) They encounter problems later.
C) They learn a new skill.
D) They receive a reward.

Answer: B) They encounter problems later.

Explanation: The character's choice to ignore advice leads to problems, illustrating the cause-and-effect relationship in the story.

---

12. What does the phrase "a tough cookie" mean?

A) A person who is very sweet
B) A person who is hard to break or defeat
C) A type of dessert
D) A type of food that is difficult to chew

Answer: B) A person who is hard to break or defeat

Explanation: The phrase "a tough cookie" is an idiom meaning a person who is strong or resilient and can handle challenges.

---

13. Which of these sentences uses figurative language?

A) The dog barked loudly.
B) She ran as fast as a cheetah.
C) The car stopped at the red light.
D) The sun was shining brightly.

Answer: B) She ran as fast as a cheetah.

Explanation: The sentence uses a simile, comparing her speed to that of a cheetah, which is an example of figurative language.

---

14. What is the most likely reason the author wrote this passage?

A) To entertain the reader with a fun story
B) To explain how to do something

C) To share facts about animals
D) To teach a lesson

Answer: A) To entertain the reader with a fun story

Explanation: The passage is written to entertain, as it tells a story rather than providing instructions or sharing facts.

---

15. What is the cause of the character feeling happy in the story?

A) They received a gift.
B) They lost a race.
C) They found something valuable.
D) They failed a test.

Answer: A) They received a gift.

Explanation: The character feels happy because they received something special, which is the cause of their happiness.

---

16. How does the author help the reader understand the character's feelings?

A) By describing the character's actions
B) By listing the character's traits
C) By using descriptive language
D) By telling the character's thoughts directly

Answer: C) By using descriptive language

Explanation: The author uses descriptive language to show the character's emotions, such as describing their facial expressions or actions.

---

17. Which of the following is a fact from the passage?

A) The dog was the fastest in the race.
B) The puppy loved to run.
C) The dog won the race because of its speed.
D) Dogs are great pets for many families.

Answer: D) Dogs are great pets for many families.

Explanation: This is a fact because it's a general statement that can be supported by evidence. The other options are more about personal experiences or opinions.

18. What is the purpose of the author's use of a question in the passage?

A) To introduce the main idea
B) To keep the reader interested
C) To explain a concept
D) To list important details

Answer: B) To keep the reader interested

Explanation: Using a question at the beginning of a passage or section is often a strategy to engage the reader and make them think about the topic.

---

19. What is a supporting detail in this sentence: "Elephants are the largest land animals and have big ears"?

A) Elephants are very friendly.
B) Elephants have big ears.
C) Elephants live in Africa.
D) Elephants can swim.

Answer: B) Elephants have big ears.

Explanation: The detail "elephants have big ears" supports the statement that elephants are large animals, providing additional information about them.

---

20. Which sentence uses correct punctuation?

A) She ran to the store to buy milk, eggs and bread.
B) She ran to the store, to buy milk, eggs and bread.
C) She ran to the store to buy milk eggs and bread.
D) She ran to the store to buy milk, eggs, and bread.

Answer: D) She ran to the store to buy milk, eggs, and bread.

Explanation: Option D correctly uses commas to separate items in a list.

---

21. What is the author's purpose in this passage? "The moon looks very bright tonight because of the clear sky."

A) To explain why the moon is bright
B) To tell a story about the moon
C) To describe the moon
D) To ask a question about the moon

Answer: A) To explain why the moon is bright

Explanation: The passage explains the reason why the moon looks bright—because the sky is clear.

---

22. What does the character do to solve the problem in the story?

A) They ask for help from a friend.
B) They give up.
C) They ignore the issue.
D) They try different solutions until one works.

Answer: D) They try different solutions until one works.

Explanation: The character does not give up but tries various solutions to overcome the problem.

---

23. Which of the following words is a compound word?

A) Dog
B) Flower
C) Playground
D) House

Answer: C) Playground

Explanation: A compound word is made up of two smaller words. "Playground" is a compound word formed from "play" and "ground."

---

24. What type of text is this? "A step-by-step guide to building a birdhouse."

A) Fiction
B) Nonfiction
C) Fantasy
D) Poetry

Answer: B) Nonfiction

Explanation: This is a nonfiction text because it provides factual information and instructions, not a story or imaginative writing.

---

25. What would happen if the character did not apologize in the story?

A) They would feel better.
B) They would make things worse.

C) They would solve the problem.
D) They would feel angry.

Answer: B) They would make things worse.

Explanation: The character's apology helps resolve the situation. Without it, the problem would likely continue.

---

26. What type of sentence is this? "I love to read books on a rainy day."

A) Statement
B) Question
C) Command
D) Exclamation

Answer: A) Statement

Explanation: The sentence makes a statement about the speaker's enjoyment of reading, rather than asking a question, giving a command, or expressing excitement.

---

27. What can you infer about the character based on their actions in the story?

A) They are very brave.
B) They are feeling sad.
C) They are trying to help others.
D) They are angry.

Answer: C) They are trying to help others.

Explanation: The character's actions show a desire to assist others, which is why option C is the best inference. Inferences are conclusions based on clues or actions in the text.

---

28. Which of the following is the theme of the story?

A) Friendship
B) Science
C) The importance of learning
D) Adventure

Answer: A) Friendship

Explanation: The theme of a story is the underlying message or central idea. If the story revolves around characters supporting each other and forming bonds, then friendship is the theme.

29. Which sentence from the passage shows that the character is scared?

A) "He looked around, his heart racing."
B) "She smiled and laughed with her friends."
C) "The sun was shining brightly."
D) "He sat calmly on the bench."

Answer: A) "He looked around, his heart racing."

Explanation: The sentence "his heart racing" shows a physical reaction to fear, indicating that the character is scared.

30. What is the purpose of using descriptive words in the story?

A) To make the story longer
B) To make the story more interesting
C) To confuse the reader
D) To make the story sound funny

Answer: B) To make the story more interesting

Explanation: Descriptive words help create a vivid picture in the reader's mind, making the story more engaging and interesting.

31. Which sentence best describes the character's point of view?

A) "I think the park is a wonderful place to visit."
B) "The park has trees and a big playground."
C) "The park is located in the middle of the city."
D) "Many people enjoy walking in the park every day."

Answer: A) "I think the park is a wonderful place to visit."

Explanation: The sentence expresses the character's opinion about the park, showing their personal point of view.

32. What does the word "giant" mean in this sentence: "The giant fish swam through the ocean"?

A) A fish that is very small
B) A fish that is very large
C) A fish that is very fast
D) A fish that is very colorful

Answer: B) A fish that is very large

Explanation: The word "giant" describes something very large, so it refers to the size of the fish in this context.

---

33. What does the author want the reader to learn from the story?

A) How to make a cake
B) The importance of kindness
C) What happens during a thunderstorm
D) How to build a house

Answer: B) The importance of kindness

Explanation: The message or lesson the author wants the reader to take away is often the theme of the story. In this case, kindness is emphasized.

---

34. What does the character do to solve the problem?

A) They ask for help from others.
B) They ignore the problem.
C) They give up right away.
D) They try to solve it alone without help.

Answer: A) They ask for help from others.

Explanation: The character resolves the issue by seeking assistance, which shows cooperation and problem-solving skills.

---

35. What is the author's purpose in describing the weather in the story?

A) To explain what the character is doing
B) To set the mood or tone of the story
C) To give facts about the weather
D) To describe the setting only

Answer: B) To set the mood or tone of the story

Explanation: Describing the weather helps set the atmosphere of the story. For example, a rainy day can create a somber or mysterious mood, affecting the tone.

---

36. What can you predict will happen next in the story?

A) The character will solve the problem.
B) The character will leave the scene.
C) The character will ask for help.
D) The character will find a new friend.

Answer: A) The character will solve the problem.

Explanation: Based on the current events and the character's actions, a logical prediction is that the character will find a solution to the problem.

---

37. What is the effect of the character's choice to help the stranger in the story?

A) The stranger becomes angry.
B) The stranger is thankful and gives a reward.
C) The character feels sad.
D) The character regrets their choice.

Answer: B) The stranger is thankful and gives a reward.

Explanation: By helping the stranger, the character experiences a positive outcome where the stranger is grateful and offers a reward.

---

38. What is a text feature that helps the reader understand the topic better?

A) Glossary
B) Chapter number
C) Page number
D) Author's name

Answer: A) Glossary

Explanation: A glossary provides definitions for unfamiliar words, helping the reader better understand the topic by explaining key terms.

---

39. Which sentence from the story shows that the character is feeling nervous?

A) "She shook her hands and looked around the room."
B) "She laughed and smiled at her friend."
C) "She skipped down the hallway with excitement."
D) "She spoke loudly and confidently to the class."

Answer: A) "She shook her hands and looked around the room."

Explanation: The action of shaking hands and looking around indicates nervousness, as it shows uncertainty or anxiety in the character.

40. How do you know that the story is about a fantasy world?

A) The story mentions magical creatures.
B) The story takes place in the real world.
C) The characters are humans.
D) The story talks about historical events.

Answer: A) The story mentions magical creatures.

Explanation: A fantasy world typically includes magical or imaginary creatures or events, which makes option A the correct choice.

41. What is the meaning of the word "explore" as used in the sentence: "The child wanted to explore the forest"?

A) To look carefully and investigate
B) To build a shelter
C) To stay in one place
D) To plant trees

Answer: A) To look carefully and investigate

Explanation: "Explore" means to search or investigate something in detail, which in this case refers to the child wanting to discover more about the forest.

42. What is the central theme of the story?

A) The importance of teamwork
B) How to solve math problems
C) The value of hard work
D) The challenges of living in space

Answer: A) The importance of teamwork

Explanation: If the story involves characters working together to achieve a common goal, the central theme will be teamwork.

43. Which of these details shows how the character feels about their new home?

A) "The house had a large garden with flowers and trees."
B) "The character walked into the house and smiled."
C) "The house was on a busy street."
D) "The house had a small living room."

Answer: B) "The character walked into the house and smiled."

Explanation: The character's smile shows that they are happy or excited about their new home, providing an emotional detail about their feelings.

---

44. Which of these is an example of a character trait?

A) He was wearing a red shirt.
B) She had long brown hair.
C) He was always kind to others.
D) She liked to read books.

Answer: C) He was always kind to others.

Explanation: Character traits describe a person's behavior or attitude. "Always kind" is a character trait, while the other options describe appearance or interests.

---

45. What is the effect of the character's decision to apologize to their friend?

A) The friend forgives the character and they continue their relationship.
B) The friend becomes angry.
C) The character feels even worse.
D) The friend ignores the character.

Answer: A) The friend forgives the character and they continue their relationship.

Explanation: The character's apology leads to forgiveness and helps repair the relationship, which is a positive outcome of apologizing.

---

46. What is the author trying to teach the reader in this story?

A) The value of honesty
B) How to bake a cake
C) The history of ancient Egypt
D) The benefits of reading

Answer: A) The value of honesty

Explanation:
The author likely uses the characters' actions and choices to emphasize the importance of being truthful, as seen through the consequences of dishonesty in the story.

---

47. Which of the following best describes the setting of the story?

A) A quiet forest with towering trees
B) A busy city with lots of people
C) A quiet room with bookshelves
D) A sunny beach with sand and water

Answer: A) A quiet forest with towering trees

Explanation:
The setting refers to where and when the story takes place. A "quiet forest with towering trees" is a detailed description that indicates the setting.

---

48. How can you tell that the character is determined to succeed?

A) They never give up, even when things are difficult.
B) They take frequent breaks.
C) They complain about their challenges.
D) They ask for help immediately.

Answer: A) They never give up, even when things are difficult.

Explanation:
Determination is shown through perseverance and the decision to keep trying despite challenges.

---

49. Which of these best describes the problem in the story?

A) The character lost their favorite toy.
B) The character is trying to find a hidden treasure.
C) The character doesn't understand a new subject in school.
D) The character is trying to make new friends.

Answer: B) The character is trying to find a hidden treasure.

Explanation:
The central problem in the story could revolve around the character's quest for treasure, making option B the most relevant.

50. What is the meaning of the word "brave" in the sentence: "The brave soldier entered the battlefield"?

A) Happy
B) Strong
C) Courageous
D) Scared

Answer: C) Courageous

Explanation:
"Brave" describes someone who has courage in difficult or dangerous situations.

---

51. What is the effect of the character finding a new friend?

A) The character is lonely.
B) The character is happy and enjoys their company.
C) The character becomes upset.
D) The character ignores them.

Answer: B) The character is happy and enjoys their company.

Explanation:
Finding a new friend generally results in happiness and companionship for the character.

---

52. Which sentence shows that the character is feeling proud?

A) "She smiled as she held her medal high."
B) "She dropped the medal on the floor."
C) "She looked disappointed and sat down."
D) "She handed the medal to her friend."

Answer: A) "She smiled as she held her medal high."

Explanation:
A smile while holding a medal shows pride in the accomplishment, indicating the character feels proud.

---

53. Which of these is the best summary of the story?

A) The main character gets lost in the forest but finds their way home.
B) A group of animals builds a treehouse together.
C) The main character makes a new friend while traveling.
D) The character solves a mystery with their detective skills.

Answer: A) The main character gets lost in the forest but finds their way home.

Explanation:
A good summary captures the main idea of the story. The character getting lost and finding their way home is a clear summary of the plot.

---

54. What does the character do after they make a mistake?

A) They apologize and try again.
B) They quit and walk away.
C) They blame others for the mistake.
D) They ignore the mistake.

Answer: A) They apologize and try again.

Explanation:
Characters who apologize and try again demonstrate resilience and accountability, which is often a positive moral in stories.

---

55. What is the purpose of the introduction in the story?

A) To introduce the characters and setting
B) To provide a moral lesson
C) To describe the problem
D) To show the story's ending

Answer: A) To introduce the characters and setting

Explanation:
The introduction sets the stage by introducing the characters, the setting, and often the main problem, giving the reader a foundation to understand the story.

---

56. Which of the following words is a synonym for "hungry"?

A) Full
B) Thirsty
C) Starving
D) Tired

Answer: C) Starving

Explanation:
"Starving" is a synonym for "hungry," meaning having a strong desire for food.

57. What can we infer about the character from their actions?

A) They are very excited about the upcoming event.
B) They are feeling embarrassed and avoid looking at others.
C) They are very happy and confident.
D) They are sad and crying.

Answer: B) They are feeling embarrassed and avoid looking at others.

Explanation:
The character's actions (avoiding eye contact) suggest that they feel embarrassed, an emotion inferred from their behavior.

---

58. Why does the author include a description of the setting?

A) To make the story more interesting and help the reader visualize the environment
B) To give factual information
C) To introduce new characters
D) To make the story longer

Answer: A) To make the story more interesting and help the reader visualize the environment

Explanation:
Descriptive settings allow readers to visualize the environment and feel more engaged in the story.

---

59. What can be concluded about the character based on their reaction to the surprise?

A) They are delighted and surprised.
B) They are angry and upset.
C) They are confused and unsure of what to do.
D) They are pleased but try to hide it.

Answer: A) They are delighted and surprised.

Explanation:
The character's reaction—expressing delight and surprise—indicates their joy and amazement.

---

60. Which of the following is an example of a character using figurative language?

A) "The moon was as bright as a diamond."
B) "She walked slowly across the room."
C) "He ate his dinner in silence."
D) "The book was very interesting."

Answer: A) "The moon was as bright as a diamond."

Explanation:
The comparison "as bright as a diamond" is a simile, a type of figurative language.

---

61. What is the author's purpose in writing a story about a character who learns from their mistakes?

A) To entertain the reader
B) To show the importance of learning from errors
C) To describe the setting
D) To explain a scientific fact

Answer: B) To show the importance of learning from errors

Explanation:
The author likely wants to teach the reader that making mistakes is part of learning and growing.

---

62. What is the meaning of the word "enormous" in the sentence: "The enormous elephant walked through the jungle"?

A) Small
B) Heavy
C) Very large
D) Slow

Answer: C) Very large

Explanation:
"Enormous" describes something very large or huge, such as the elephant in the sentence.

---

63. What does the character do to solve the problem in the story?

A) They ask for advice from their friend.
B) They ignore the problem and walk away.
C) They give up immediately.
D) They try to solve it on their own without help.

Answer: A) They ask for advice from their friend.

Explanation:
Asking for help is often a way characters solve problems in a story, showing teamwork and collaboration.

---

64. How does the author create suspense in the story?

A) By using short, quick sentences to keep the reader engaged
B) By describing the setting in detail
C) By revealing the ending early in the story
D) By introducing a happy event early on

Answer: A) By using short, quick sentences to keep the reader engaged

Explanation:
Short, rapid sentences create urgency and tension, which builds suspense as the reader anticipates what will happen next.

---

65. What is the main idea of the passage?

A) The importance of healthy eating
B) A character's journey to find treasure
C) The main character learns a valuable lesson
D) The history of an ancient civilization

Answer: C) The main character learns a valuable lesson

Explanation:
The main idea of the passage is often focused on the lesson learned by the character, which is the central message of the story.

---

66. What is the best way to summarize the story?

A) A character finds a magical object that changes their life.
B) A character learns a lesson and helps others along the way.
C) A character runs into trouble and escapes.
D) A character visits a new country and has fun.

Answer: B) A character learns a lesson and helps others along the way.

Explanation:
A good summary captures the essence of the story, highlighting the lessons and character growth.

67. What does the character feel after they achieve their goal?

A) Disappointed
B) Proud and accomplished
C) Confused
D) Tired and sad

Answer: B) Proud and accomplished

Explanation:
After achieving a goal, characters often feel proud, demonstrating success and satisfaction.

---

68. Why is the title of the story important?

A) It gives the reader a hint about the main idea.
B) It is just for decoration.
C) It includes the name of the main character.
D) It is a quote from the story.

Answer: A) It gives the reader a hint about the main idea.

Explanation:
The title often provides a preview of the central theme or plot of the story, making it easier for the reader to understand.

---

69. How does the character change from the beginning to the end of the story?

A) They become more confident and brave.
B) They stay the same throughout.
C) They become less interested in the problem.
D) They become sadder and less hopeful.

Answer: A) They become more confident and brave.

Explanation:
Character growth and change are common in stories, often leading to increased confidence or bravery by the end.

---

70. What does the character learn by the end of the story?

A) That they can always solve their problems on their own
B) That they should never trust anyone

C) That teamwork is important
D) That being quiet is the best way to make friends

Answer: C) That teamwork is important

Explanation:
Many stories emphasize the value of working together with others to solve problems and achieve goals.

---

71. What does the word "glistening" mean in the sentence: "The snow was glistening in the sunlight"?

A) Bright and shiny
B) Cold and wet
C) Soft and fluffy
D) Heavy and dark

Answer: A) Bright and shiny

Explanation:
"Glistening" describes something shining or sparkling, especially due to light reflecting off its surface, such as snow in sunlight.

---

72. How can you tell that the character is feeling worried?

A) The character smiles and laughs.
B) The character fidgets and looks around nervously.
C) The character sings a song.
D) The character sits quietly with their eyes closed.

Answer: B) The character fidgets and looks around nervously.

Explanation:
Signs of worry often include nervous habits like fidgeting and looking around, indicating anxiety or concern.

---

73. What is the main problem in the story?

A) The character is trying to find a lost pet.
B) The character wants to win a race.
C) The character has to move to a new town.
D) The character is afraid of the dark.

Answer: A) The character is trying to find a lost pet.

Explanation:
The main problem often involves a challenge or goal the character is trying to overcome, such as finding a lost pet.

---

74. What does the character decide to do when faced with a challenge?

A) The character gives up.
B) The character seeks help from others.
C) The character runs away.
D) The character ignores the problem.

Answer: B) The character seeks help from others.

Explanation:
Seeking help is a positive way characters often respond to challenges, showing teamwork and resourcefulness.

---

75. Which of these events happens first in the story?

A) The character wins a prize.
B) The character faces a big decision.
C) The character helps a friend.
D) The character solves a mystery.

Answer: B) The character faces a big decision.

Explanation:
The beginning of a story often introduces a decision that drives the plot forward, making it the first key event.

---

76. Which sentence from the story shows that the character is excited?

A) "The character jumped up and down with joy."
B) "The character sighed and looked away."
C) "The character quietly sat down."
D) "The character frowned and crossed their arms."

Answer: A) "The character jumped up and down with joy."

Explanation:
Jumping up and down with joy shows a high level of excitement and happiness.

77. What is the meaning of the word "predict" in the sentence: "Can you predict what will happen next?"

A) Guess
B) Write
C) Forget
D) Read

Answer: A) Guess

Explanation:
"Predict" means to guess or estimate what will happen in the future based on clues or information.

---

78. What lesson does the character learn by the end of the story?

A) That being kind to others is important
B) That taking shortcuts is always the best option
C) That it's okay to give up on challenges
D) That being dishonest can help you win

Answer: A) That being kind to others is important

Explanation:
The lesson in stories often revolves around positive traits like kindness and honesty, showing the importance of treating others well.

---

79. Why does the character feel sad in the story?

A) They lost their favorite toy.
B) They found out a secret about their friend.
C) They didn't win a race they worked hard for.
D) They were left out of a fun activity.

Answer: D) They were left out of a fun activity.

Explanation:
Feeling left out is a common reason for sadness, especially when a character is excluded from something enjoyable.

---

80. What is the best description of the character's personality?

A) They are shy and quiet.
B) They are adventurous and brave.

C) They are angry and upset.
D) They are quiet and serious.

Answer: B) They are adventurous and brave.

Explanation:
The character's actions, such as taking risks or exploring, reveal their adventurous and brave nature.

---

81. How does the author describe the character's emotions in the story?

A) Through actions and words they say
B) Through the setting and weather
C) Through other characters' opinions
D) Through the objects they interact with

Answer: A) Through actions and words they say

Explanation:
Authors often show a character's emotions by describing their actions and dialogue, which help reveal their inner feelings.

---

82. What is the best way to summarize the passage?

A) The character travels to a new country.
B) The character solves a problem with the help of a friend.
C) The character learns a lesson about kindness.
D) The character goes on an adventure to find treasure.

Answer: C) The character learns a lesson about kindness.

Explanation:
Summarizing the passage means identifying the key lesson or theme of the story, in this case, kindness.

---

83. Why does the character choose to apologize in the story?

A) They want to make up for a mistake they made.
B) They are too tired to continue.
C) They want to avoid getting in trouble.
D) They do not care about the situation.

Answer: A) They want to make up for a mistake they made.

Explanation:
Apologizing usually occurs when a character wants to make amends for a mistake and restore peace.

---

84. What makes the character in the story a hero?

A) They always follow the rules.
B) They help others without expecting anything in return.
C) They are always the strongest in the group.
D) They never get scared or worried.

Answer: B) They help others without expecting anything in return.

Explanation:
A hero is often someone who acts selflessly to help others, making option B the best choice.

---

85. Which of these is an example of a character using problem-solving skills?

A) The character draws a picture to explain a situation.
B) The character asks a friend for help with a difficult task.
C) The character tries several ways to fix a broken toy.
D) The character ignores the problem and walks away.

Answer: C) The character tries several ways to fix a broken toy.

Explanation:
Problem-solving often involves trying different solutions, as shown in the character's attempts to fix the toy.

---

86. What does the character want to achieve in the story?

A) To travel to a new city
B) To win a race and earn a prize
C) To make a new friend
D) To find a hidden treasure

Answer: B) To win a race and earn a prize

Explanation:
The character's goal is often a key part of the plot, such as winning a race, which drives their actions.

---

87. What type of character is the main character in the story?

A) Heroic and brave
B) Shy and quiet
C) Lazy and disinterested
D) Curious and adventurous

Answer: D) Curious and adventurous

Explanation:
A curious and adventurous character often seeks new experiences and learns valuable lessons along the way.

---

88. Which word describes the character's feelings after receiving a compliment?

A) Embarrassed
B) Angry
C) Proud
D) Confused

Answer: C) Proud

Explanation:
Receiving a compliment often leads to feelings of pride and happiness, as the character is recognized for their actions.

---

89. What is the cause of the problem in the story?

A) The character lost a pet.
B) The character has a bad attitude.
C) The character needs to complete a difficult task.
D) The character is in a new environment.

Answer: D) The character is in a new environment.

Explanation:
Being in a new environment can create challenges for a character, such as feelings of confusion or loneliness.

---

90. How does the character feel at the end of the story?

A) Confused and unsure
B) Proud and satisfied
C) Angry and frustrated
D) Sad and disappointed

Answer: B) Proud and satisfied

Explanation:
At the end of a story, the character often feels a sense of accomplishment or fulfillment after overcoming challenges.

---

91. What does the word "sturdy" mean in the sentence: "The sturdy tree stood tall in the forest"?

A) Weak
B) Strong
C) Flexible
D) Small

Answer: B) Strong

Explanation:
"Sturdy" means strong and able to endure, like a tree that stands tall against the wind.

---

92. How does the setting contribute to the mood of the story?

A) The setting is dark and gloomy, creating a sense of fear.
B) The setting is bright and cheerful, making the reader feel happy.
C) The setting is quiet and peaceful, leading to a calm mood.
D) The setting is cold and harsh, making the reader feel anxious.

Answer: B) The setting is bright and cheerful, making the reader feel happy.

Explanation:
A cheerful setting can create an uplifting mood for the reader, contributing to a positive atmosphere in the story.

---

93. What does the character do to solve the problem in the story?

A) They ask for help from a friend.
B) They ignore the problem and hope it goes away.
C) They work alone and try different solutions.
D) They give up and accept defeat.

Answer: C) They work alone and try different solutions.

Explanation:
In many stories, characters work independently and explore multiple solutions to overcome challenges.

94. What is the best summary of the story?

A) The character learns the value of friendship and teamwork.
B) The character is on an exciting adventure and finds treasure.
C) The character faces challenges and becomes more confident.
D) The character wins a prize after a long journey.

Answer: A) The character learns the value of friendship and teamwork.

Explanation:
Summarizing the key message or lesson of a story, such as the importance of teamwork, helps capture its essence.

95. How does the character change after learning an important lesson?

A) They become more understanding and patient.
B) They become angry and upset.
C) They ignore the lesson and continue as before.
D) They become less interested in their goals.

Answer: A) They become more understanding and patient.

Explanation:
Learning an important lesson often leads to positive personal growth, like becoming more understanding and patient.

96. What clue in the story helps you figure out the character's feelings?

A) The character's actions and words
B) The setting and background music
C) The other characters' reactions
D) The colors used in the illustrations

Answer: A) The character's actions and words

Explanation:
Actions and dialogue are strong indicators of how a character feels in the story.

97. What is the meaning of the word "familiar" in the sentence: "The place looked familiar to me"?

A) Strange
B) Uncomfortable

C) Known or recognized
D) New

Answer: C) Known or recognized

Explanation:
"Familiar" means something that is known or has been seen before, making it easy to recognize.

---

98. Which word best describes the character's reaction when they see something surprising?

A) Nervous
B) Excited
C) Shocked
D) Bored

Answer: C) Shocked

Explanation:
A shocked reaction typically involves surprise or disbelief, which is often shown in stories when something unexpected happens.

---

99. What happens in the middle of the story?

A) The main character faces a major challenge.
B) The character finds a hidden treasure.
C) The character makes a new friend.
D) The character learns a new skill.

Answer: A) The main character faces a major challenge.

Explanation:
In most stories, the middle part introduces a challenge or problem the main character must overcome.

---

100. How does the character show their courage in the story?

A) By helping a friend in need
B) By avoiding a difficult situation
C) By refusing to take any risks
D) By choosing to stay quiet

Answer: A) By helping a friend in need

Explanation:
Courage is often shown when a character faces a difficult situation head-on, often to help someone else in need.

---

101. What does the word "delighted" mean in the sentence: "She was delighted with her birthday gift"?

A) Angry
B) Very happy
C) Tired
D) Disappointed

Answer: B) Very happy

Explanation:
"Delighted" means feeling very happy or pleased, especially with something received or experienced.

---

102. Which of these events happens at the end of the story?

A) The character learns an important lesson.
B) The character starts a new adventure.
C) The character finds a treasure.
D) The character helps a friend.

Answer: A) The character learns an important lesson.

Explanation:
The end of a story usually focuses on resolving the problem and the character learning a lesson or gaining wisdom.

---

103. What is the main theme of the story?

A) The importance of hard work and dedication
B) The adventure of finding treasure
C) The importance of being kind and helpful
D) The excitement of a new friendship

Answer: C) The importance of being kind and helpful

Explanation:
The theme of a story often reflects the key lesson the characters learn, such as kindness and helping others.

104. What does the word "gloomy" mean in the sentence: "The sky was gloomy before the rain"?

A) Sunny
B) Bright
C) Dark and sad
D) Clear

Answer: C) Dark and sad

Explanation:
"Gloomy" describes a mood or setting that is dark, sad, or depressing, like overcast skies before rain.

---

105. How does the character show they are determined?

A) By giving up on their goal
B) By not letting challenges stop them
C) By avoiding all risks
D) By asking others to do the hard work

Answer: B) By not letting challenges stop them

Explanation:
Determined characters continue working toward their goals despite challenges, showing persistence and resolve.

---

106. What does the character do when they face a tough decision?

A) They ask for advice from others.
B) They ignore the decision and hope it goes away.
C) They make the decision quickly without thinking.
D) They give up and accept whatever happens.

Answer: A) They ask for advice from others.

Explanation:
When faced with a tough decision, characters often seek advice from others to make a more informed choice.

---

107. Which part of the story shows the character's fear?

A) The character stands tall and faces the challenge.
B) The character hides from the problem.
C) The character bravely speaks up.
D) The character smiles and laughs.

Answer: B) The character hides from the problem.

Explanation:
Fear often causes characters to avoid facing challenges or problems, as shown when they hide or withdraw.

---

108. What is the character's main goal in the story?

A) To find a treasure
B) To help someone in need
C) To learn a new skill
D) To solve a mystery

Answer: B) To help someone in need

Explanation:
Many stories focus on the character's desire to help others, which drives their actions and decisions.

---

109. What is the lesson the character learns by the end of the story?

A) That they can always avoid problems
B) That facing challenges makes them stronger
C) That money is the most important thing
D) That running away is the best solution

Answer: B) That facing challenges makes them stronger

Explanation:
The character often grows and learns from overcoming challenges, showing that resilience leads to personal strength.

---

110. What does the word "enthusiastic" mean in the sentence: "She was enthusiastic about the new book"?

A) Sad
B) Excited
C) Nervous
D) Indifferent

Answer: B) Excited

Explanation:
"Enthusiastic" describes being very excited and eager about something, such as a new book.

---

111. Which of these best describes the story's setting?

A) A dark forest
B) A sunny beach
C) A busy city street
D) A quiet school classroom

Answer: A) A dark forest

Explanation:
The setting of a story can greatly influence its tone. A dark forest suggests mystery or adventure.

---

112. Why does the character feel proud?

A) Because they overcame a difficult challenge
B) Because they lost a race
C) Because they didn't try hard enough
D) Because they were praised for something easy

Answer: A) Because they overcame a difficult challenge

Explanation:
Pride often results from overcoming a difficult task, showing the character's sense of achievement.

---

113. What is the problem the character faces in the story?

A) They lose their favorite toy.
B) They need to find their way home.
C) They have to learn a new skill.
D) They don't get along with their sibling.

Answer: B) They need to find their way home.

Explanation:
A common problem in stories involves characters trying to overcome obstacles or finding their way home after getting lost.

114. What does the word "reluctant" mean in the sentence: "The character was reluctant to speak in front of the class"?

A) Eager
B) Unwilling
C) Brave
D) Excited

Answer: B) Unwilling

Explanation:
"Reluctant" means unwilling or hesitant to do something, in this case, speaking in front of the class.

115. What is the most likely reason the character decided to help?

A) They wanted to make a friend.
B) They were asked to help.
C) They knew it was the right thing to do.
D) They needed a favor in return.

Answer: C) They knew it was the right thing to do.

Explanation:
Helping others is often driven by a strong sense of right and wrong, not by expectations of rewards or favors.

116. How do we know the character is feeling frustrated?

A) They smile and laugh.
B) They sigh and look disappointed.
C) They cheer and jump up and down.
D) They sing a happy song.

Answer: B) They sigh and look disappointed.

Explanation:
Frustration is often shown by a sigh, a disappointed look, or actions that show the character is upset.

117. What is the primary challenge the character faces?

A) Finding a new friend
B) Learning how to read
C) Solving a puzzle
D) Overcoming their fear

Answer: D) Overcoming their fear

Explanation:
Many stories revolve around characters learning to overcome their fears, whether it's fear of the dark, speaking in front of others, or facing something unknown.

---

118. What motivates the character to keep going despite challenges?

A) A desire to win a prize
B) A desire to impress others
C) A sense of responsibility or duty
D) A need for fame

Answer: C) A sense of responsibility or duty

Explanation:
When characters feel a sense of responsibility, they are often motivated to continue working toward their goal despite obstacles.

---

119. What is the best description of the story's theme?

A) The importance of honesty and trust
B) The excitement of exploring new places
C) The value of hard work and perseverance
D) The joy of spending time with friends

Answer: A) The importance of honesty and trust

Explanation:
A theme often reflects the central idea or lesson of the story. In this case, it highlights honesty and trust.

---

120. What does the character do to show they are brave?

A) They make a difficult decision despite their fears.
B) They refuse to take any risks.
C) They ignore the problem and hope it will go away.
D) They ask others to do the difficult tasks.

Answer: A) They make a difficult decision despite their fears.

Explanation:
Bravery often involves making tough decisions or taking action despite feeling afraid or uncertain.

---

121. How does the character feel about their decision?

A) Happy and satisfied
B) Regretful and unsure
C) Angry and upset
D) Confused and lost

Answer: A) Happy and satisfied

Explanation:
Feeling happy and satisfied with a decision often indicates that the character feels good about the choice they made.

---

122. Which word in the sentence shows the character is feeling tired?

"She yawned and rubbed her eyes as she finished her homework."

A) Yawned
B) Rubbing
C) Finished
D) Eyes

Answer: A) Yawned

Explanation:
"Yawned" suggests that the character is feeling tired or sleepy.

---

123. What does the word "grateful" mean in the sentence: "She was grateful for the help her friend gave her"?

A) Angry
B) Thankful
C) Confused
D) Nervous

Answer: B) Thankful

Explanation:
"Grateful" means feeling thankful or appreciative for something that was done for you.

124. What is the setting of the story?

A) A castle in a faraway land
B) A busy city street
C) A small village in the mountains
D) A house by the beach

Answer: C) A small village in the mountains

Explanation:
The setting of a story is where and when the story takes place. In this case, it is a small village in the mountains.

---

125. Why does the character feel nervous in the story?

A) They are about to speak in front of the class.
B) They are meeting a new friend.
C) They are going on a vacation.
D) They are eating their favorite food.

Answer: A) They are about to speak in front of the class.

Explanation:
Speaking in front of the class can make people feel nervous due to the attention and pressure.

---

126. How does the character change by the end of the story?

A) They become more confident.
B) They decide to give up on their dream.
C) They stop trying to help others.
D) They get more frustrated.

Answer: A) They become more confident.

Explanation:
Character development often involves growth, such as becoming more confident after overcoming challenges.

---

127. What is the lesson the character learns?

A) That it's okay to be afraid of challenges.
B) That they should never try new things.

C) That asking for help can make things easier.
D) That they are always right.

Answer: C) That asking for help can make things easier.

Explanation:
The lesson the character learns is that reaching out to others for help can make difficult tasks more manageable.

---

128. What does the word "eager" mean in the sentence: "He was eager to begin his new project"?

A) Hesitant
B) Excited
C) Bored
D) Confused

Answer: B) Excited

Explanation:
"Eager" means very excited and ready to do something, as shown in this sentence.

---

129. What happens first in the story?

A) The character makes a decision.
B) The character faces a challenge.
C) The character has a problem.
D) The character learns a lesson.

Answer: C) The character has a problem.

Explanation:
Typically, the first part of a story introduces the problem or challenge the main character will deal with.

---

130. Why does the character refuse to give up?

A) Because they want to prove others wrong
B) Because they believe they can succeed
C) Because they are afraid to fail
D) Because they want a reward

Answer: B) Because they believe they can succeed

Explanation:
The character's refusal to give up often stems from a belief in their ability to succeed despite obstacles.

---

131. What word describes the character's excitement about the event?

A) Nervous
B) Thrilled
C) Worried
D) Tired

Answer: B) Thrilled

Explanation:
"Thrilled" describes a high level of excitement or happiness about something that is happening.

---

132. What is the main reason the character feels disappointed?

A) They didn't get what they expected.
B) They won a prize.
C) They learned something new.
D) They met a new friend.

Answer: A) They didn't get what they expected.

Explanation:
Disappointment often happens when expectations are not met or something doesn't go as planned.

---

133. Which part of the story shows the character's kindness?

A) The character helps someone who is in trouble.
B) The character refuses to share.
C) The character ignores someone asking for help.
D) The character decides to leave a situation.

Answer: A) The character helps someone who is in trouble.

Explanation:
Kindness is shown when a character offers assistance or shows empathy to others in need.

---

134. What does the character do to fix their mistake?

A) They apologize and make it right.
B) They ignore it and move on.
C) They blame someone else.
D) They get upset and walk away.

Answer: A) They apologize and make it right.

Explanation:
Fixing a mistake often involves acknowledging it and taking responsibility to correct it.

---

135. What is the main idea of the story?

A) A character explores new places.
B) A character learns how to solve a problem.
C) A character goes on an adventure.
D) A character makes a new friend.

Answer: B) A character learns how to solve a problem.

Explanation:
The main idea of many stories centers on solving problems or overcoming challenges.

---

136. Why does the character feel proud of their actions?

A) Because they helped someone in need
B) Because they ran away from the situation
C) Because they gave up
D) Because they did nothing

Answer: A) Because they helped someone in need

Explanation:
Pride often comes from doing something meaningful or helpful to others, such as offering assistance when needed.

---

137. Which word in the sentence suggests the character is worried?

"Her hands shook as she opened the letter."

A) Shook
B) Opened
C) Letter
D) Hands

Answer: A) Shook

Explanation:
"Shook" often indicates nervousness or worry, especially in a tense moment like opening an important letter.

---

138. How does the character feel at the end of the story?

A) Confused
B) Satisfied
C) Angry
D) Nervous

Answer: B) Satisfied

Explanation:
At the end of the story, characters often feel satisfied after they have resolved their problems or completed their goals.

---

139. Which sentence shows how the character is feeling nervous?

A) "She smiled brightly as she spoke."
B) "She quickly walked away without saying anything."
C) "She stood up tall and spoke clearly."
D) "She laughed and felt excited."

Answer: B) "She quickly walked away without saying anything."

Explanation:
Nervousness is often shown through avoidance or hesitation, as in the character walking away quickly without speaking.

---

140. What is the problem the character faces in the story?

A) The character needs to learn a new skill.
B) The character needs to find something they lost.
C) The character needs to solve a mystery.
D) The character needs to save a friend.

Answer: B) The character needs to find something they lost.

Explanation:
Losing something important often becomes a key problem in many stories that characters need to solve.

141. What does the word "content" mean in the sentence: "The dog seemed content after playing outside"?

A) Angry
B) Tired
C) Happy and satisfied
D) Nervous

Answer: C) Happy and satisfied

Explanation:
"Content" means being happy and satisfied with what one has, as shown in this context about the dog.

---

142. Why does the character decide to take a risk?

A) Because they are bored
B) Because they want to prove something
C) Because they believe it will help someone
D) Because they want to avoid facing a problem

Answer: C) Because they believe it will help someone

Explanation:
Characters often take risks to help others, driven by a sense of responsibility or care for the people around them.

---

143. What is the lesson the character learns by the end of the story?

A) That being brave is always easy
B) That helping others is important
C) That they should always be afraid
D) That they should always give up

Answer: B) That helping others is important

Explanation:
The lesson of a story often teaches values such as kindness, bravery, or the importance of helping others.

---

144. Which part of the story shows that the character is afraid?

A) The character smiles at the challenge.
B) The character decides to face their fear.

C) The character hides from the problem.
D) The character boldly steps forward.

Answer: C) The character hides from the problem.

Explanation:
Fear often leads characters to avoid situations or hide from the problem, rather than confronting it directly.

---

145. What is the character's goal in the story?

A) To win a competition
B) To make a new friend
C) To solve a mystery
D) To find something important

Answer: D) To find something important

Explanation:
The goal of a story is often the main mission or challenge the character is trying to accomplish.

---

146. What is the tone of the story?

A) Happy
B) Scary
C) Exciting
D) Sad

Answer: C) Exciting

Explanation:
Tone refers to the overall mood or feeling of the story, and an exciting tone often involves thrilling or suspenseful events.

---

147. How does the character feel after they reach their goal?

A) Exhausted
B) Relieved
C) Angry
D) Disappointed

Answer: B) Relieved

Explanation:
Reaching a goal often brings a sense of relief, especially after facing challenges or obstacles.

---

148. Why does the character act quickly?

A) Because they want to show off
B) Because they need to solve a problem fast
C) Because they are not interested in the outcome
D) Because they have plenty of time

Answer: B) Because they need to solve a problem fast

Explanation:
Characters often act quickly when there is a sense of urgency or a need to solve a problem in a short amount of time.

---

149. How does the setting influence the story?

A) The setting makes the character feel safe.
B) The setting makes the character feel afraid.
C) The setting is not important to the story.
D) The setting helps the character achieve their goals.

Answer: B) The setting makes the character feel afraid.

Explanation:
Sometimes the setting can create a mood that affects how the character feels, such as feeling scared in a dark forest.

---

150. What makes the character decide to keep going?

A) The support from others
B) Their fear of failure
C) The excitement of success
D) The desire for a reward

Answer: A) The support from others

Explanation:
Support from friends or family can be a strong motivator, encouraging characters to continue even when challenges arise.

151. What does the word "curious" mean in the sentence: "The boy was curious about the new book in the library"?

A) Scared
B) Interested and eager to learn
C) Bored
D) Confused

Answer: B) Interested and eager to learn

Explanation:
"Curious" refers to a strong desire to learn or find out about something.

---

152. What can you infer about the character from the sentence: "She hurried to the door, hoping she wasn't too late"?

A) She is in a hurry.
B) She is relaxed and calm.
C) She is excited about her plans.
D) She is confused.

Answer: A) She is in a hurry.

Explanation:
The word "hurried" indicates that the character is rushing to get somewhere or do something quickly.

---

153. How does the character react to the challenge in the story?

A) They give up without trying.
B) They accept it and try their best.
C) They are afraid and refuse to do anything.
D) They ignore the challenge completely.

Answer: B) They accept it and try their best.

Explanation:
In many stories, characters grow by facing challenges and trying their best to overcome them.

---

154. What is the purpose of the character's action in the sentence: "He raised his hand to ask a question"?

A) To show he's bored
B) To get attention
C) To participate in the conversation
D) To leave the room

Answer: C) To participate in the conversation

Explanation:
Raising a hand is a common action for participating and asking questions in a classroom setting.

---

155. Why is the character feeling happy?

A) Because they won a prize.
B) Because they got in trouble.
C) Because they lost something.
D) Because they solved a difficult problem.

Answer: D) Because they solved a difficult problem.

Explanation:
Characters often feel happy when they successfully solve a problem or achieve something important.

---

156. What does the character's action reveal about them?

A) They are calm and collected.
B) They are nervous and unsure.
C) They are excited and eager.
D) They are indifferent and uninterested.

Answer: B) They are nervous and unsure.

Explanation:
The way a character acts can show their emotions or state of mind, such as feeling nervous and unsure.

---

157. What happens when the character faces a setback?

A) They keep going and try again.
B) They give up and quit.
C) They blame others.
D) They ignore the problem.

Answer: A) They keep going and try again.

Explanation:
Overcoming setbacks often involves persistence and continuing to try, even when things don't go as planned.

---

158. What does the word "reluctant" mean in the sentence: "He was reluctant to speak in front of the class"?

A) Excited
B) Unwilling
C) Confident
D) Joyful

Answer: B) Unwilling

Explanation:
"Reluctant" means being hesitant or unwilling to do something, often due to fear or uncertainty.

---

159. Why does the character feel proud in the story?

A) They helped someone in need.
B) They ignored the situation.
C) They did not try their best.
D) They did not finish their task.

Answer: A) They helped someone in need.

Explanation:
Characters often feel proud when they do something kind, such as helping others.

---

160. What lesson can be learned from the story?

A) That it's okay to quit when things get hard.
B) That helping others is important.
C) That it's good to be selfish.
D) That it's better to ignore problems.

Answer: B) That helping others is important.

Explanation:
The lesson of many stories often emphasizes kindness, helping others, and making a positive impact.

161. How does the character feel after winning the race?

A) Angry
B) Proud and happy
C) Nervous
D) Sad

Answer: B) Proud and happy

Explanation:
Winning a race or achieving something is often associated with feelings of pride and happiness.

162. What does the character do when they are in trouble?

A) They ask for help.
B) They ignore the problem.
C) They run away.
D) They give up immediately.

Answer: A) They ask for help.

Explanation:
Asking for help is a common and important action when characters face difficulties in stories.

163. Why does the character choose to act bravely?

A) Because they are not afraid
B) Because they want to impress others
C) Because they want to do what is right
D) Because they don't know what to do

Answer: C) Because they want to do what is right

Explanation:
Characters often act bravely because they believe in doing the right thing, even when it's difficult.

164. What does the word "surprised" mean in the sentence: "She was surprised by the unexpected gift"?

A) Happy and excited
B) Disappointed

C) Confused and shocked
D) Sad

Answer: C) Confused and shocked

Explanation:
"Surprised" refers to a feeling of shock or unexpected reaction to something that wasn't anticipated.

---

165. What is the main problem the character faces?

A) They can't find their way home.
B) They don't have enough time to finish a task.
C) They are lost in the woods.
D) They are stuck in a difficult situation.

Answer: D) They are stuck in a difficult situation.

Explanation:
The main problem often involves a difficult situation the character needs to resolve, such as being stuck or facing a challenge.

---

166. How does the character feel when they accomplish their goal?

A) Disappointed
B) Relieved and happy
C) Nervous
D) Sad

Answer: B) Relieved and happy

Explanation:
After reaching a goal, characters typically feel a sense of relief and happiness from their achievement.

---

167. Why does the character hesitate to speak up?

A) Because they are scared of being wrong
B) Because they don't care
C) Because they are excited
D) Because they are happy

Answer: A) Because they are scared of being wrong

Explanation:
Hesitation to speak is often due to fear of making mistakes or saying the wrong thing.

---

168. What is the main reason the character feels frustrated?

A) They have too much homework.
B) They can't find something important.
C) They are stuck in a bad situation.
D) They can't make a decision.

Answer: C) They are stuck in a bad situation.

Explanation:
Frustration often arises when a character feels stuck or unable to resolve a problem.

---

169. What is the main lesson the character learns?

A) That it's okay to quit when it's hard
B) That being kind to others is important
C) That it's better to stay alone
D) That it's good to be selfish

Answer: B) That being kind to others is important

Explanation:
Many stories teach lessons about kindness and helping others as an important value.

---

170. What does the character do to show their friendship?

A) They share something special.
B) They ignore their friend.
C) They criticize their friend.
D) They stay away from their friend.

Answer: A) They share something special.

Explanation:
Friendship is often shown through acts of kindness, such as sharing something important or meaningful.

---

171. What does the word "confident" mean in the sentence: "She felt confident during her presentation"?

A) Nervous
B) Sure of herself
C) Sad
D) Confused

Answer: B) Sure of herself

Explanation:
"Confident" means feeling sure of oneself, especially when facing challenges or tasks.

---

172. What motivates the character to keep going?

A) A desire to win
B) A need to prove something to others
C) The support of a friend
D) A fear of failure

Answer: C) The support of a friend

Explanation:
Characters are often motivated by the encouragement or support of others when facing challenges.

---

173. How does the character change by the end of the story?

A) They become more confident.
B) They give up their goals.
C) They become angry.
D) They stop trying.

Answer: A) They become more confident.

Explanation:
Character development often shows growth, such as increased confidence or self-assurance.

---

174. What does the character want most in the story?

A) To be left alone
B) To help others
C) To succeed or win
D) To escape their problems

Answer: C) To succeed or win

Explanation:
Many stories involve a character's desire to achieve success or reach a goal.

---

175. Why does the character decide to help?

A) Because they feel sorry for someone
B) Because they want something in return
C) Because they want to be kind
D) Because they are forced to

Answer: C) Because they want to be kind

Explanation:
Helping others is often motivated by kindness, without expecting anything in return.

---

176. What is the most important lesson the character learns?

A) That it's okay to ignore problems
B) That helping others makes a difference
C) That staying angry helps solve problems
D) That winning is the only thing that matters

Answer: B) That helping others makes a difference

Explanation:
Characters often learn the value of kindness and how it can positively impact others.

---

177. What does the character find in the end?

A) A hidden treasure
B) A friend
C) A solution to their problem
D) A new adventure

Answer: C) A solution to their problem

Explanation:
In many stories, characters discover a solution after overcoming obstacles or challenges.

---

178. Why is the character so excited?

A) They won a prize.
B) They are going on an adventure.

C) They solved a big problem.
D) They met a new friend.

Answer: B) They are going on an adventure.

Explanation:
Excitement is often linked to the anticipation of a new and exciting experience or journey.

---

179. What does the character feel when they lose something important?

A) Angry
B) Sad and worried
C) Happy
D) Confused

Answer: B) Sad and worried

Explanation:
Losing something important typically brings feelings of sadness or concern about what's been lost.

---

180. What motivates the character to keep trying, despite failures?

A) They are determined to succeed.
B) They want to prove others wrong.
C) They are afraid of failing.
D) They don't care about the outcome.

Answer: A) They are determined to succeed.

Explanation:
Characters often keep trying because they are determined to overcome difficulties and reach their goal.

---

181. What is the main reason the character feels afraid in the story?

A) They are lost in a dark forest.
B) They are meeting new people.
C) They are excited about an upcoming event.
D) They are playing with their pet.

Answer: A) They are lost in a dark forest.

Explanation:
Fear often arises from unfamiliar or dangerous situations, such as being lost.

182. How does the character show they are sorry for their actions?

A) They ignore the situation.
B) They apologize and try to make things right.
C) They blame someone else.
D) They act like nothing happened.

Answer: B) They apologize and try to make things right.

Explanation:
Apologizing and trying to correct the mistake shows that the character is remorseful.

183. What does the word "adventure" mean in the sentence: "The group went on an exciting adventure"?

A) A boring trip
B) A dangerous and thrilling experience
C) A peaceful walk
D) A sad journey

Answer: B) A dangerous and thrilling experience

Explanation:
"Adventure" refers to an exciting or risky experience that often involves exploring new places or situations.

184. What is the most important goal of the character in the story?

A) To win a prize
B) To help others
C) To explore new places
D) To solve a mystery

Answer: D) To solve a mystery

Explanation:
The character's goal may involve solving a problem or uncovering answers to unknowns.

185. How does the character feel when they see their friend after a long time?

A) Sad
B) Angry

C) Excited and happy
D) Nervous

Answer: C) Excited and happy

Explanation:
Meeting a friend after a long time often brings feelings of joy and excitement.

---

186. What does the word "gigantic" mean in the sentence: "The gigantic tree towered over the forest"?

A) Tiny
B) Very small
C) Very large
D) Old and weak

Answer: C) Very large

Explanation:
"Gigantic" means extremely large or enormous.

---

187. Why does the character decide to keep their promise?

A) Because they fear punishment
B) Because they want to make things right
C) Because they want attention
D) Because they are too tired to change their mind

Answer: B) Because they want to make things right

Explanation:
Characters often keep promises because they value trust and want to honor their word.

---

188. What motivates the character to take action in the story?

A) The need to impress others
B) The desire to help a friend
C) The fear of getting in trouble
D) The excitement of a reward

Answer: B) The desire to help a friend

Explanation:
Motivation can stem from wanting to help others, especially friends in need.

189. What does the word "distracted" mean in the sentence: "She was distracted by the noise outside"?

A) Focused and alert
B) Confused and unsure
C) Unable to focus because of something else
D) Happy and relaxed

Answer: C) Unable to focus because of something else

Explanation:
"Distracted" means being unable to concentrate because something else is drawing attention.

---

190. What lesson can be learned from the character's actions?

A) That it's good to always follow rules
B) That being kind to others is important
C) That winning is the most important thing
D) That it's okay to cheat

Answer: B) That being kind to others is important

Explanation:
Many stories focus on kindness as an important lesson to teach.

---

191. What does the character do when they feel overwhelmed?

A) They take a break and ask for help.
B) They ignore the problem.
C) They give up right away.
D) They argue with others.

Answer: A) They take a break and ask for help.

Explanation:
When feeling overwhelmed, taking a break and asking for help can be a helpful solution.

---

192. Why does the character feel proud of themselves?

A) They finished a difficult task.
B) They avoided the situation.

C) They ignored others' needs.
D) They didn't try their best.

Answer: A) They finished a difficult task.

Explanation:
Pride often comes from overcoming challenges or successfully completing tasks.

---

193. What does the character do when they don't understand something?

A) They ignore it.
B) They ask questions to learn more.
C) They complain about it.
D) They pretend to understand.

Answer: B) They ask questions to learn more.

Explanation:
Asking questions is a good strategy when something is unclear or hard to understand.

---

194. What can you infer about the character from the sentence: "She jumped in excitement when she saw the surprise"?

A) She is upset.
B) She is confused.
C) She is very happy.
D) She is scared.

Answer: C) She is very happy.

Explanation:
Jumping in excitement typically shows happiness and enthusiasm.

---

195. How does the character feel when they are surrounded by friends?

A) Lonely
B) Nervous
C) Comfortable and happy
D) Angry

Answer: C) Comfortable and happy

Explanation:
Being around friends often brings comfort and happiness.

196. What does the word "whispered" mean in the sentence: "He whispered so no one could hear him"?

A) Shouted loudly
B) Spoke in a quiet voice
C) Spoke with excitement
D) Said nothing

Answer: B) Spoke in a quiet voice

Explanation:
"Whispered" means to speak in a soft voice, often so others can't hear.

197. Why does the character get frustrated?

A) They cannot find what they are looking for.
B) They win a game.
C) They help someone in need.
D) They make a new friend.

Answer: A) They cannot find what they are looking for.

Explanation:
Frustration often occurs when a person cannot find something important or solve a problem.

198. What is the character's reaction when they learn new information?

A) They are confused and unsure.
B) They are interested and curious.
C) They ignore it.
D) They get upset.

Answer: B) They are interested and curious.

Explanation:
Learning new things often sparks curiosity and interest.

199. What is the purpose of the character's action in the sentence: "She saved her money to buy a gift for her friend"?

A) To waste time
B) To make her friend happy

C) To buy something for herself
D) To impress her family

Answer: B) To make her friend happy

Explanation:
Saving money to buy a gift for someone else shows thoughtfulness and kindness.

---

200. How does the character feel after they help someone?

A) Sad
B) Proud and happy
C) Angry
D) Nervous

Answer: B) Proud and happy

Explanation:
Helping others often makes characters feel proud and satisfied.

---

201. What does the word "grateful" mean in the sentence: "She felt grateful for her friend's help"?

A) Disappointed
B) Thankful and appreciative
C) Confused
D) Angry

Answer: B) Thankful and appreciative

Explanation:
"Grateful" means feeling thankful and appreciative for something kind or helpful.

---

202. Why does the character feel unsure about their decision?

A) They have a lot of confidence.
B) They don't have enough information.
C) They are excited about the choice.
D) They are determined to stick to their plan.

Answer: B) They don't have enough information.

Explanation:
Uncertainty often comes from a lack of information or clarity about a decision.

203. What can you infer about the character from their actions?

A) They are uninterested.
B) They are helpful and caring.
C) They are rude and mean.
D) They are confused.

Answer: B) They are helpful and caring.

Explanation:
Actions that show kindness or assistance often indicate that the character is caring.

204. What is the character's attitude toward the challenge they face?

A) They are afraid to try.
B) They are determined to succeed.
C) They ignore the challenge.
D) They are bored.

Answer: B) They are determined to succeed.

Explanation:
A determined attitude helps characters overcome challenges and obstacles.

205. How does the character respond when they see a problem?

A) They avoid it.
B) They try to fix it right away.
C) They complain about it.
D) They ignore the problem.

Answer: B) They try to fix it right away.

Explanation:
Proactive characters respond by attempting to solve problems as soon as they arise.

206. What does the word "stubborn" mean in the sentence: "He was stubborn and refused to change his mind"?

A) Willing to change
B) Difficult to deal with
C) Not willing to change
D) Happy to listen

Answer: C) Not willing to change

Explanation:
"Stubborn" describes someone who refuses to change their opinion or action.

---

207. What is the main reason the character feels nervous?

A) They are going on an exciting adventure.
B) They are meeting someone new.
C) They are about to perform in front of others.
D) They have an important decision to make.

Answer: C) They are about to perform in front of others.

Explanation:
Nervousness often arises when facing situations that involve performance or public speaking.

---

208. How does the character show their excitement?

A) By staying quiet
B) By jumping up and down
C) By frowning
D) By walking away

Answer: B) By jumping up and down

Explanation:
Physical expressions, like jumping, can show excitement or enthusiasm.

---

209. What does the word "shiny" mean in the sentence: "The shiny car reflected the sunlight"?

A) Dull and dark
B) Smooth and rough
C) Bright and reflecting light
D) Rusty and old

Answer: C) Bright and reflecting light

Explanation:
"Shiny" means something is bright and reflects light, often due to being polished or new.

210. Why does the character smile when they see a gift?

A) They are surprised and happy.
B) They are disappointed.
C) They don't like gifts.
D) They are confused.

Answer: A) They are surprised and happy.

Explanation:
Receiving a gift usually brings feelings of joy and surprise.

---

211. What is the main reason the character chooses to leave home?

A) They want to explore new places.
B) They are unhappy at home.
C) They are looking for treasure.
D) They are meeting a friend.

Answer: A) They want to explore new places.

Explanation:
The character is motivated by a desire for exploration and adventure.

---

212. What does the word "familiar" mean in the sentence: "The familiar smell of cookies filled the house"?

A) Strange and unknown
B) Well known and recognized
C) New and different
D) Bad and unpleasant

Answer: B) Well known and recognized

Explanation:
"Familiar" means something that is known or recognized from previous experiences.

---

213. Why is the character feeling nervous in the story?

A) They are about to face a test.
B) They are meeting someone new.
C) They have lost something important.
D) They are going to a party.

Answer: A) They are about to face a test.

Explanation:
Feeling nervous is common before important events like tests or challenges.

---

214. What is the character's reaction when they receive a surprise gift?

A) They are upset and confused.
B) They are happy and grateful.
C) They ignore the gift.
D) They are angry and disappointed.

Answer: B) They are happy and grateful.

Explanation:
Receiving a gift often brings feelings of joy and appreciation.

---

215. What can be inferred about the character from their actions?

A) They are selfish and only care about themselves.
B) They are brave and willing to help others.
C) They are always sad and worried.
D) They are uninterested in their surroundings.

Answer: B) They are brave and willing to help others.

Explanation:
Helping others is often a sign of bravery and kindness.

---

216. How does the character feel about going to a new school?

A) Excited and eager
B) Scared and nervous
C) Angry and frustrated
D) Confused and lost

Answer: B) Scared and nervous

Explanation:
Starting something new, like a school, can make someone feel nervous.

---

217. What does the word "relaxed" mean in the sentence: "She felt relaxed on the beach, listening to the waves"?

A) Anxious and worried
B) Calm and at ease
C) Restless and unable to sleep
D) Tired and sleepy

Answer: B) Calm and at ease

Explanation:
"Relaxed" means feeling calm and free from stress.

---

218. Why does the character help the injured animal?

A) Because they are scared of it
B) Because they feel sorry for it
C) Because they want attention
D) Because they want a reward

Answer: B) Because they feel sorry for it

Explanation:
Helping someone or something out of compassion is a sign of empathy.

---

219. How does the character react when they make a mistake?

A) They ignore it and keep going.
B) They apologize and try to fix it.
C) They laugh it off and move on.
D) They blame someone else.

Answer: B) They apologize and try to fix it.

Explanation:
Apologizing and taking responsibility for mistakes shows maturity.

---

220. What can you infer about the setting of the story based on the description of the weather?

A) It is sunny and warm.
B) It is cold and rainy.
C) It is dark and stormy.
D) It is foggy and mysterious.

Answer: B) It is cold and rainy.

Explanation:
Descriptions of weather can set the tone and atmosphere of the story.

---

221. What does the character do when they feel sad?

A) They talk to a friend about their feelings.
B) They ignore their feelings and pretend to be happy.
C) They make others feel sad too.
D) They try to solve everyone else's problems.

Answer: A) They talk to a friend about their feelings.

Explanation:
Talking about emotions can help people process and deal with sadness.

---

222. Why does the character keep trying even though they keep failing?

A) They believe they will eventually succeed.
B) They are afraid of failing in front of others.
C) They don't care if they succeed or not.
D) They want to give up but feel they have to continue.

Answer: A) They believe they will eventually succeed.

Explanation:
Persistence often comes from the belief that success is possible through effort.

---

223. How does the character show they are nervous about something?

A) They laugh loudly.
B) They avoid looking at anyone.
C) They sit still and fidget.
D) They shout and act confidently.

Answer: C) They sit still and fidget.

Explanation:
Nervousness is often shown through fidgeting or avoiding eye contact.

---

224. What is the character's main goal in the story?

A) To find a hidden treasure.
B) To win a race.

C) To help someone in need.
D) To escape from danger.

Answer: C) To help someone in need.

Explanation:
Many characters' goals revolve around assisting others and making a positive impact.

---

225. What does the character do when they feel excited?

A) They run around shouting.
B) They stay calm and quiet.
C) They share the news with others.
D) They ignore their excitement.

Answer: C) They share the news with others.

Explanation:
Excitement often leads to sharing good news with others.

---

226. What lesson can be learned from the character's actions?

A) Never trust anyone.
B) It's important to be patient and wait for the right time.
C) Being mean is always the best choice.
D) Winning is the most important thing.

Answer: B) It's important to be patient and wait for the right time.

Explanation:
Patience and timing are valuable lessons, often learned through the character's journey.

---

227. Why is the character feeling proud of themselves?

A) They finished a hard task.
B) They were praised by others.
C) They made a mistake and learned from it.
D) They didn't try at all.

Answer: A) They finished a hard task.

Explanation:
Accomplishing something challenging can make a character feel proud of their effort.

228. What does the word "disappointed" mean in the sentence: "He was disappointed when he didn't win the game"?

A) Excited and happy
B) Sad and let down
C) Confused and unsure
D) Angry and upset

Answer: B) Sad and let down

Explanation:
"Disappointed" refers to feeling sad or let down when expectations aren't met.

---

229. How does the character react when they achieve their goal?

A) They celebrate and thank everyone.
B) They feel guilty for succeeding.
C) They ignore the success.
D) They are upset and disappointed.

Answer: A) They celebrate and thank everyone.

Explanation:
Achieving a goal often leads to celebrations and gratitude for the support received.

---

230. Why does the character feel embarrassed?

A) They made a mistake in front of others.
B) They won a prize.
C) They helped someone in need.
D) They had a great idea.

Answer: A) They made a mistake in front of others.

Explanation:
Embarrassment often comes from doing something in public that one feels self-conscious about.

---

231. What is the character's attitude towards helping others?

A) They only help when they have to.
B) They enjoy helping others and do it willingly.
C) They avoid helping anyone.
D) They help others for rewards.

Answer: B) They enjoy helping others and do it willingly.

Explanation:
A positive attitude toward helping others is often a sign of empathy and kindness.

---

232. Why does the character feel confident in their decision?

A) They have a lot of experience.
B) They are familiar with the situation.
C) They asked for advice from others.
D) They are ignoring others' opinions.

Answer: B) They are familiar with the situation.

Explanation:
Confidence can stem from experience or knowledge about a situation.

---

233. How does the character feel after solving the problem?

A) Relieved and satisfied
B) More confused
C) Angry and upset
D) Disappointed

Answer: A) Relieved and satisfied

Explanation:
Solving a problem often brings relief and a sense of accomplishment.

---

234. What does the word "brave" mean in the sentence: "The brave knight fought the dragon to protect the village"?

A) Scared
B) Courageous and willing to face danger
C) Lazy and uninterested
D) Nervous and afraid

Answer: B) Courageous and willing to face danger

Explanation:
"Brave" describes someone who is willing to face dangerous or difficult situations.

---

235. How does the character feel about their decision to speak up?

A) They regret it and feel embarrassed.
B) They feel proud and confident.
C) They wish they had kept quiet.
D) They are unsure about what to do next.

Answer: B) They feel proud and confident.

Explanation:
Speaking up can lead to feelings of pride when the character stands up for what they believe.

---

236. Why is the character upset after hearing the news?

A) The news was unexpected and difficult to hear.
B) The news was exactly what they wanted to hear.
C) The news made them feel excited.
D) The news made them laugh.

Answer: A) The news was unexpected and difficult to hear.

Explanation:
News that surprises or shocks the character can lead to feelings of upset or sadness.

---

237. What does the word "delicious" mean in the sentence: "The delicious cake smelled amazing"?

A) Smelly and bad
B) Tasty and enjoyable
C) Bitter and unpleasant
D) Sour and hard to eat

Answer: B) Tasty and enjoyable

Explanation:
"Delicious" means something that is very tasty or enjoyable to eat.

---

238. Why does the character apologize?

A) They want to make the situation better.
B) They don't care about the situation.
C) They want to avoid being punished.
D) They feel embarrassed.

Answer: A) They want to make the situation better.

Explanation:
Apologizing is often a way to show regret and improve a situation.

239. How does the character show that they are excited about something?

A) By speaking softly
B) By smiling and jumping
C) By looking away
D) By sitting still

Answer: B) By smiling and jumping

Explanation:
Excitement is often shown through visible actions like smiling or jumping up and down.

240. Why is the character surprised when they open the gift?

A) The gift is exactly what they wanted.
B) The gift is much bigger than expected.
C) The gift is unexpected and unusual.
D) The gift is broken.

Answer: C) The gift is unexpected and unusual.

Explanation:
Surprise often comes from receiving something unexpected or out of the ordinary.

241. What does the character do when they feel proud of their achievement?

A) They ignore it and keep working.
B) They celebrate with their friends.
C) They cry because they are overwhelmed.
D) They ask for a reward.

Answer: B) They celebrate with their friends.

Explanation:
Celebrating achievements with others shows pride and happiness.

242. Why does the character help the lost dog?

A) They are trying to impress someone.
B) They want to keep the dog as a pet.

C) They feel sorry for the dog.
D) They are afraid of being scolded.

Answer: C) They feel sorry for the dog.

Explanation:
Helping others out of compassion is often driven by empathy.

---

243. How does the character feel when they win the race?

A) They feel sad.
B) They feel proud and happy.
C) They feel angry.
D) They feel confused.

Answer: B) They feel proud and happy.

Explanation:
Winning a race often brings feelings of pride and accomplishment.

---

244. What is the character's main goal in the story?

A) To find a treasure.
B) To make a new friend.
C) To overcome their fear.
D) To win a competition.

Answer: C) To overcome their fear.

Explanation:
The character's goal is often to face challenges and grow.

---

245. What does the word "nervous" mean in the sentence: "She felt nervous before giving the speech"?

A) Relaxed and calm
B) Excited and happy
C) Worried and uneasy
D) Confused and lost

Answer: C) Worried and uneasy

Explanation:
"Nervous" refers to feeling anxious or uneasy about something.

246. What does the character do to show that they are feeling sorry?

A) They ignore the situation.
B) They apologize and try to fix their mistake.
C) They laugh and walk away.
D) They blame someone else.

Answer: B) They apologize and try to fix their mistake.

Explanation:
Apologizing and taking responsibility for mistakes shows maturity.

247. Why does the character feel relieved at the end of the story?

A) They have solved the problem.
B) They have made a new friend.
C) They have won a contest.
D) They have received a reward.

Answer: A) They have solved the problem.

Explanation:
Relief often comes after solving a difficult situation or overcoming a challenge.

248. How does the character react when they are given a compliment?

A) They ignore it and walk away.
B) They blush and smile.
C) They get embarrassed and upset.
D) They feel angry and annoyed.

Answer: B) They blush and smile.

Explanation:
Receiving a compliment often causes a person to feel pleased and happy.

249. What does the character do when they see someone in trouble?

A) They ignore the situation.
B) They ask for help.
C) They laugh at the person.
D) They try to help the person.

Answer: D) They try to help the person.

Explanation:
Helping others is a sign of kindness and empathy.

---

250. How does the character feel when they receive bad news?

A) Happy and excited
B) Angry and upset
C) Sad and disappointed
D) Confused and unsure

Answer: C) Sad and disappointed

Explanation:
Bad news often leads to feelings of sadness and disappointment.

---

251. Why does the character feel excited about the upcoming event?

A) They have been waiting for it for a long time.
B) They are worried about what will happen.
C) They are unsure about it.
D) They have to prepare for something difficult.

Answer: A) They have been waiting for it for a long time.

Explanation:
Excitement often comes from anticipation of something they are looking forward to.

---

252. What does the character do when they feel nervous?

A) They run away.
B) They stay calm and breathe deeply.
C) They shout and get angry.
D) They ask others for help.

Answer: B) They stay calm and breathe deeply.

Explanation:
Nervousness can often be eased by taking deep breaths and staying calm.

---

253. What is the main lesson the character learns in the story?

A) It's important to always be right.
B) Teamwork is better than working alone.
C) Money is the most important thing.
D) Never trust anyone.

Answer: B) Teamwork is better than working alone.

Explanation:
Working with others can help achieve a goal faster and more efficiently.

---

254. How does the character feel after helping someone in need?

A) Angry and upset
B) Proud and happy
C) Confused and unsure
D) Sad and worried

Answer: B) Proud and happy

Explanation:
Helping others often brings feelings of pride and satisfaction.

---

255. What does the word "adventure" mean in the sentence: "They went on an exciting adventure in the forest"?

A) A boring and uneventful trip
B) A thrilling and exciting experience
C) A simple walk through the park
D) A stressful and frightening journey

Answer: B) A thrilling and exciting experience

Explanation:
"Adventure" refers to an exciting or unusual experience, often involving exploration.

---

256. Why does the character feel scared during the storm?

A) They are afraid of the dark.
B) They are afraid of the loud noises and wind.
C) They are worried about missing the storm.
D) They are excited about the weather.

Answer: B) They are afraid of the loud noises and wind.

Explanation:
Storms can be frightening because of the loud noises and unpredictable weather.

257. How does the character show kindness to others?

A) By ignoring their problems
B) By helping them when they are in need
C) By taking things from them
D) By being rude and unkind

Answer: B) By helping them when they are in need

Explanation:
Kindness is shown through helpful actions and consideration for others.

258. What does the word "scared" mean in the sentence: "She felt scared when she heard strange noises"?

A) Excited and curious
B) Nervous and anxious
C) Brave and confident
D) Confused and lost

Answer: B) Nervous and anxious

Explanation:
"Scared" means feeling fearful or anxious about something unknown or frightening.

259. Why does the character feel disappointed after the event?

A) They did not win as they expected.
B) They were surprised by the outcome.
C) They enjoyed the event despite not winning.
D) They were happy with the results.

Answer: A) They did not win as they expected.

Explanation:
Disappointment can occur when things don't turn out as hoped or expected.

260. What is the character's main challenge in the story?

A) Learning to ride a bike
B) Finding a hidden treasure
C) Overcoming their fear of the dark
D) Winning a race

Answer: C) Overcoming their fear of the dark

Explanation:
Facing fears is often a central challenge in many stories.

---

261. What does the character learn from their experience?

A) It's better to give up when things get hard.
B) Helping others is rewarding.
C) It's best to keep everything to yourself.
D) Winning is all that matters.

Answer: B) Helping others is rewarding.

Explanation:
Helping others can provide emotional rewards and teach valuable lessons.

---

262. How does the character feel when they see their friends succeed?

A) Jealous and upset
B) Proud and happy for them
C) Angry and frustrated
D) Indifferent and bored

Answer: B) Proud and happy for them

Explanation:
Feeling happy for others' success is a sign of empathy and kindness.

---

263. Why is the character excited to go on the trip?

A) They are looking forward to seeing new places.
B) They are nervous about traveling.
C) They are unsure of where they are going.
D) They are worried about the journey.

Answer: A) They are looking forward to seeing new places.

Explanation:
Excitement for a trip often comes from the anticipation of new experiences.

264. What is the character's attitude when they face a tough situation?

A) They give up quickly.
B) They stay positive and try to solve the problem.
C) They complain and do nothing.
D) They blame others for their problems.

Answer: B) They stay positive and try to solve the problem.

Explanation:
A positive attitude helps in overcoming challenges and finding solutions.

---

265. What does the word "mysterious" mean in the sentence: "The mysterious door led to a hidden room"?

A) Boring and uninteresting
B) Unknown and hard to explain
C) Bright and colorful
D) Loud and noisy

Answer: B) Unknown and hard to explain

Explanation:
"Mysterious" refers to something that is difficult to understand or explain.

---

266. Why does the character feel proud after finishing the project?

A) They completed the task on their own.
B) They received a reward for their work.
C) They helped someone else finish it.
D) They took a long time to finish.

Answer: A) They completed the task on their own.

Explanation:
Accomplishing something independently often brings feelings of pride.

---

267. How does the character respond to a challenge in the story?

A) They ignore it.
B) They face it bravely and with determination.
C) They get upset and cry.
D) They ask for help immediately.

Answer: B) They face it bravely and with determination.

Explanation:
Facing challenges with courage shows inner strength and perseverance.

---

268. Why does the character feel thankful at the end of the story?

A) They were given something important.
B) They made new friends.
C) They learned something valuable.
D) They won a competition.

Answer: C) They learned something valuable.

Explanation:
Gratitude often comes from gaining knowledge or life lessons.

---

269. What is the character's main feeling during the storm?

A) Calm and relaxed
B) Excited and happy
C) Scared and worried
D) Angry and frustrated

Answer: C) Scared and worried

Explanation:
Storms often cause fear and anxiety due to their unpredictability.

---

270. How does the character feel when they are praised for their efforts?

A) Embarrassed and uncomfortable
B) Proud and appreciated
C) Angry and frustrated
D) Confused and unsure

Answer: B) Proud and appreciated

Explanation:
Praise for hard work or efforts often boosts self-esteem and confidence.

---

271. What does the character do when they feel nervous about the test?

A) They study harder and focus.
B) They give up and refuse to try.
C) They get angry and upset.
D) They complain to others.

Answer: A) They study harder and focus.

Explanation:
Being nervous can motivate the character to work harder and prepare.

---

272. Why does the character decide to help their friend in the story?

A) They are scared to be alone.
B) They want to prove they are better.
C) They care about their friend's feelings.
D) They think they will get something in return.

Answer: C) They care about their friend's feelings.

Explanation:
True friendship involves helping others because you care.

---

273. How does the character feel when they are unable to find their favorite toy?

A) Excited and happy
B) Sad and disappointed
C) Angry and frustrated
D) Confused and unsure

Answer: B) Sad and disappointed

Explanation:
Losing something special often leads to feelings of sadness.

---

274. What does the character do when they find a treasure map?

A) They ignore it and walk away.
B) They try to follow the map and find the treasure.
C) They give it to someone else.
D) They hide it from others.

Answer: B) They try to follow the map and find the treasure.

Explanation:
Finding a treasure map often leads to an adventure or discovery.

Made in United States
Orlando, FL
04 February 2025